Sharon Neill was at college when she discovered that she could communicate with the dead. She began to hone her talents by practising readings on her friends and, after working as a receptionist and doing readings in her own time, she eventually became a full-time medium. She now regularly tours the country and her events sell out within a matter of days. She has appeared on various television shows and lives in Belfast. Visit her website at www.sharon-neill.com.

Second Sight

SHARON NEILL

An Orion paperback

First published in Great Britain in 2007
by Orion Books
This paperback edition published in 2008
by Orion Books Ltd,
Orion House, 5 Upper St Martin's Lane,
London WC2H 9EA

An Hachette Livre UK company

1 3 5 7 9 10 8 6 4 2

A CIP catalogue record for this book is available
from the British Library.

ISBN 978-0-7528-9358-7

Printed and bound in the UK by CPI Mackays, Chatham ME5 8TD

The Orion Publishing Group's policy is to use papers that
are natural, renewable and recyclable products and
made from wood grown in sustainable forests. The logging
and manufacturing processes are expected to conform to
the environmental regulations of the country of origin.

www.orionbooks.co.uk

Contents

Acknowledgements

I would like to take this opportunity to thank everyone who has helped, supported and encouraged me on my life's journey – everyone who has been there for me when I needed it. Special thanks go to my manager John McStravick for his words of inspiration and sound advice, and to his family for their friendship over the years.

Significant among those who have helped me are the people I have come across in the spirit world, and in particular my spirit team, who have played a key part in my life, guiding me through the many challenges and never letting me down. I wouldn't be where I am today, nor could I have written this, without their help.

My gratitude goes also to my family for their love and care when I was growing up and for their support when I was starting out on my psychic journey, especially all the Nelson family who have always stood by me.

I am particularly grateful to all the friends who stuck with me through good times and bad, especially Richard Griffith who was my manager in the UK and his wife Helen.

It's been a pleasure to work with Amanda Harris, Lorraine Baxter, Clare Wallis, Emma Wallace, Poppy Berry, Gaby Young, Lisa Milton and all the team at Orion on this book, as well as with Gordon Wise at Curtis Brown, and of course John McStravick. And thank you to all of you, and your friends in spirit, who have shared your stories with me, and allowed me to share them with others.

Last but by no means least, I would like to thank Julie McStravick and her daughters for reading the first draft of *Second Sight* and for their invaluable help.

Prologue

——✳——

Monday – the most tedious day of the school week. We had assembly every morning, but on Monday this was rounded off by compulsory hymn singing. Don't get me wrong, I loved singing, and music has been a constant source of pleasure and comfort to me over the years, but back when I was eleven years old, it was the religious aspect of singing hymns that grated.

Despite the high sectarian profile of Northern Ireland in the 1970s due to the Troubles, religion didn't mean very much to me or to most of the other children at school, and we regarded the singing of hymns as a complete waste of time.

How I wished for heavy traffic, or even a small riot on my way in from East Belfast, so that I would miss it!

But every cloud has a silver lining and that first morning of the week was the perfect opportunity for the day pupils at Jordanstown School, like me, to catch up with our friends who were boarders. Jordanstown was (and still is) a non-denominational school for the deaf and sight impaired and we kids were all to one degree or another disabled in hearing or sight, our conditions ranging from comparatively mild to total and irreparable loss. I was completely blind.

I had a close circle of friends, many of whom I travelled to school on the bus with, but three of my best friends were weekly boarders and lived some distance from me, so that by Monday we would be bursting to tell each other what we had done over the weekend, the television programmes we'd listened to, the places we'd visited, the clothes we'd bought, even which bomb had gone off where and how much damage it had done – this was all part of growing up in the province.

That particular Monday, Sue, one of my closest friends and totally blind too, plumped herself down beside me. We hadn't spoken since Friday and I was looking forward to a chat.

'Hi, Sue,' I greeted her.

'Sammy took an overdose at the weekend.'

It was the most awful news. Sammy was her brother and the family was a very close-knit one. I felt for her hand and squeezed it.

'That's terrible, Sue,' I said. 'Has he recovered? Is he going to be OK?'

Sue started back with a gasp of astonishment – if I had been sighted I would have seen her jaw drop. 'How did you know about Sammy, Sharon?'

'You just told me!' I said in surprise.

'No I didn't. I was going to, but you never gave me the chance.'

It was my turn for my jaw to drop. I couldn't understand. She *must* have told me about Sammy – there was no way I could have known otherwise.

What was happening to me? Whose voice had it been? Something very strange was going on.

CHAPTER 1

Miracle Baby

—*—

I was born in Belfast on 22 July 1965, twelve weeks earlier than I was due, a wee scrap of a thing weighing in at 2 pounds 11 ounces. Miraculously, and to the amazement of the doctors and my mother, I survived.

My grandmother – my mother's mother – had been rushed to hospital with appendicitis, and the doctors had said it was touch and go as to whether she would come through the operation because she was overweight. When my mother heard this she went into shock and then into premature labour.

I was immediately put into an incubator for six weeks, where my weight plummeted to 2 pounds 1 ounce. The doctors didn't hold out much hope for me, but against all the odds I fought back.

At that time, the medical profession didn't realise that premature babies, who need extra oxygen for their lungs, should be blindfolded because the pure oxygen is toxic to their eyes. Like most premature babies, my eyes were not fully grown and without anything covering them, the optic nerves were burnt by the oxygen in the incubator, resulting in retinopathy of prematurity – damage to the developing blood vessels supplying the retina of the eye. Nobody knew whether the effect on my sight would be partial or complete, temporary or permanent.

Even when I was eventually allowed out of hospital I wasn't out of the woods. Until the age of three, I had frequent attacks of pneumonia, and although I can't remember any of these episodes, I apparently had a few more early brushes with death. In addition to these early setbacks, I couldn't keep any solids down until I was about eighteen months old – in fact all I *could* keep down was tinned Carnation Milk and water. The first solid food I ate was a spoonful of boiled egg beaten up in a cup with butter. The doctors never really found out what the problem was and put it down to my being premature.

But I have been extraordinarily lucky. Throughout my life, the right people have always appeared when I most needed help, and this was the case from quite early on. Ella, my grandmother, was so concerned about the constant chest infections and my frailty that she contacted a divine healer, a Mr Hare, who she had heard of through the local Methodist church, where he worked as a lay preacher and healer. She had already taken me to the famous evangelist healer Lesley Hale, but to no avail. Mr Hare proved to be instrumental in my recovery from the pneumonia and played an important role in other aspects of my well-being.

Divine healing is now better known as faith healing. Mr Hare believed that his faith in God would be strong enough to heal me – obviously, I was too young to have any beliefs at that time – and he would put his hands on me and pray over me. His strong belief worked.

During one of the attacks of pneumonia, the doctors had prepared my mother and the family for the worst, warning them that I might not last the night. So my grandmother rang Mr Hare and asked him to come to the Royal Victoria Hospital in Belfast where I had been taken. They wouldn't allow anyone in to see me except for close family, but my grandmother managed to persuade the sister in charge of the ward to let Mr Hare carry out more healing on me. Once again the healing worked, and the next morning the doctor phoned to say that I was ready to come home. The doctors couldn't understand what had taken place.

Although I was old enough to walk by that stage, for no apparent medical reason my legs would not function as they were supposed to and I stolidly resisted putting my feet on the ground. Again Mr Hare worked on me, declaring, after he had completed the healing, that my legs would be as strong as a footballer's. Immediately, I was able to start crawling. He also told my family that I would be able to see. My family knew that my eyes were damaged and, at the time, they took Mr Hare's comment to mean that my sight would improve.

All in all Mr Hare played a big part in my early life and I have much to thank him for. He has passed on, but I am certain that he takes a particular interest in what happened to little Sharon Neill and is proud of what I have achieved.

*

I come from a family of four children: two boys and two girls (including me). As I write, my brother Stephen is forty-three; I am the second child, aged forty-two; then Tracey, thirty-three; and finally James who is thirty. Tracey and James are actually my stepbrother and stepsister as my mother, Evelyn, got married again, to my stepfather, Jim Clarke. My brother Stephen chose to change his name and, like our stepsiblings, is a Clarke, but I have kept my father, James 'Hector' Neill's, surname.

My parents got divorced when I was a toddler though I know very little about the circumstances surrounding the break-up as I didn't live with my parents. The decision was taken early on in my life to place me with my grandmother, since my mum had to work and I needed full-time attention because I was so small and frail. So, effectively, my brother Stephen and I were brought up by Granny (my mum's mother) and Grandpa, surrounded by aunties. Sure, I saw quite a good deal of my mum, during the week and at the weekends, but it meant that the relationship with my mother was not as close as the one with my grandparents and aunts, and Mum took little part in my upbringing. This had various consequences for me later on, either because she didn't feel able to or didn't want to become involved in family matters that affected me. She had a variety of jobs, including working in a fibreglass factory, domestic work, selling wallpaper and paint, and finally nursing, though she is retired now due to ill health.

I used to see my father from time to time, at Christmases and on birthdays, but we lost touch in 2000 when I moved away from the family home. Although the tension and hostility surrounding this event affected my relationship with the rest of the family, there was no animosity between my father and me. We simply never got in touch with each other after I moved.

✳

I was about two when Granny first suspected I was completely blind. I responded to sound, taste, smell and touch, but she noticed that I wasn't following movement or shadows. The GP thought that I might be a slow developer, but referred me to a consultant at the ophthalmology department of the Royal

Victoria Hospital. The consultant's diagnosis was to the point.

'Well, Mrs Neill, you will have to accept that your daughter is totally and irretrievably blind,' he told my mother baldly. The news came as a terrible shock to my family.

But my blindness didn't bother me, and despite growing up during the Troubles in Northern Ireland, mine was a very happy childhood. My grandparents lived in a terraced house in South Belfast on a street called Conduit Street, which is a strange coincidence considering what I do now (a conduit is a channel or a means of communication). The River Conduit flows beneath the street to meet the Black Staff River, which in turn flows into the River Lagan.

Granny's home was the hub of the family and everyone gathered there on Saturdays. She had six daughters, three of whom were married and three who were still living with my grandparents – Roberta, Isobel and Janet. My grandfather, Robert (Bobby as he was known), was good with his hands and had built a bathroom at the back of the house, so we were better off than most of the neighbours who only had an outside toilet.

Although our house was full, it was fun and there was a great community spirit in the street, where all the neighbours got on well with each other. I have been told that I used to go to the corner shop on my bike, with one hand on the handlebar and the other feeling along the fence. I was quite safe – everyone knew me, and I would identify them not just by voice but by touching their faces with my fingers.

✳

This touching of faces seems odd to me now as I wouldn't dream of doing that any more. People sometimes ask me if I want to touch their face to identify them. This may well have been the way blind people were taught years ago, and it is certainly the way films portray blind people identifying others, but for me a person's voice is usually all I need in order to 'see' who I am talking to.

The voice is like a face to me. When a sighted person looks at someone they usually form an image of the shape of the face, eye colour, hair colour and so on. As a result sighted people are inclined to judge others by how they look and to rely on a visual impression rather than on what the person may have to say. I'm not distracted by any of these outward signs when I'm talking to someone, and my experience has taught me to judge people, usually pretty accurately, by what they are saying, the sound of their voice, and what is inside. Appearances can be very deceptive: a person who looks like a tramp might be very wise and a good deal more intelligent than a person who wears designer clothing.

People put great emphasis, too, on age and size, which never ceases to astonish me. When I'm with friends or family, I'm always amazed by the way they comment to each other on passers-by: 'Look at her! Mutton dressed as lamb!' 'Hasn't that woman got any mirrors in her house?' When I ask what they're talking about, they'll describe a woman who is overweight and scantily dressed or wearing a short skirt or brightly coloured clothing. Of course, fat, thin or badly dressed means nothing to me, so I never make these kinds of judgements about people.

Yet I have to bear in mind that this has implications for the way I dress and might be judged, and there are obvious problems here for people who are blind or partially sighted. Thankfully, my granny and aunts always chose my clothing when I was young, and made sure that what I was wearing matched and looked right. Nowadays I depend on my cousin Elizabeth, friends and shop assistants to choose the correct clothes for me, although I do have an idea of what material I like to wear – preferably something that doesn't need ironing! There are so many things that sighted people take for granted, among them ironing, which can be really tricky if you are blind – it isn't easy to feel whether the creases have been ironed out or not. When I come back from a trip and unpack, I make sure everything is placed on certain hangers in my wardrobe. This way I know by feel which T-shirts and trousers will match.

✳

When the Troubles began in August 1969, I had just turned four. Intense sectarian rioting broke out in Northern Ireland during the Orange Order's marching season, culminating in confrontations between the Catholics and the Protestants and the police, and resulting in a number of deaths. As children, we couldn't understand any of it, but as I grew older I had more of an insight into what was going on than most of the kids who lived nearby. This was because I went to a special school for the blind and deaf, which was integrated, that is to say the children there came from both Catholic and Protestant families.

This was unusual as Catholics and Protestants were mainly educated separately, their respective churches requiring the children to be taught apart because of the differences in religious beliefs. This segregation was widespread throughout the community in Northern Ireland, each religion sticking to its own patch. It's still like that now, although there are more mixed areas.

I was collected for school by bus at around 8 a.m. and didn't get home until 4 p.m. School started at 9 a.m. with assembly and finished at 3.15 p.m., but how quickly we got home depended on the traffic. If there was trouble or rioting in the centre of Belfast it was always a bonus because lessons had to stop and we had to leave early. Then there were the bomb drills. A siren would blast out, and when the teacher gave the word we had to line up by the classroom door and go to the playground. Thankfully, there was never a real bomb in the school.

The Troubles didn't affect my friendships at school at all, and while I was in primary we never really talked about them. This seems surprising to me now. There were times when we had to drive through riots to collect pupils from different parts of Belfast and had to get down on to the floor of the school bus for safety's sake. Stones, bottles and petrol bombs were thrown at rival factions or at the police, but miraculously, the windows of the school bus were never broken and no one was ever hurt. Nor can I remember feeling traumatised or frightened by what was happening; it was something we grew up with so we didn't know any different. And, of course, we used to think it was fun if we got out of school early.

Catholic and Protestant children were taught together, except when it came to religious education, when their different theological traditions meant that they were separated. I didn't question any of this while I was in primary school. We played and interacted like any other children and although the Troubles in Belfast were sometimes disruptive, we took it all in our stride.

During the 1970s and 1980s the news bulletins were not censored. They were very graphic, and when the news was on at home we kids were sent out of the living room – myself included, even though I couldn't see the pictures. I used to strain to hear what was being broadcast but rarely picked up what the items were about, though I do know that pictures were shown of people being rescued from bomb explosions and bodies being put into body bags. My grandmother wanted us out of the room in case the scenes gave us nightmares.

Our only close encounter with an explosion was when a launderette at the top of the street in South Belfast got blown up.

There was a massive bang, the reek of smoke, the sound of sirens and general chaos. The only casualties, thank goodness, were the washing machines and drinks machines that were blown into the air. In 1972, we moved to East Belfast. This was a quieter part of the city, usually spared the sectarian strife that erupted elsewhere.

However, there were frequent reminders that we weren't living in normal times. In 1974 the Ulster Workers' Council called a strike. Although I was only nine, I can remember the events vividly. The Belfast estates were barricaded, which prevented supplies of milk and other essentials from getting through to residents, and the electricity supply was disrupted across the province so we had regular power cuts. We had to cook on primus stoves or build bonfires in the back gardens. I used to find the power cuts more entertaining than the rest of the family because I could cope perfectly well in the dark and would often be given the job of going to fetch candles and other necessities.

✳

From the very start of my life, when the *Belfast Telegraph* ran a story about my premature birth headlined 'Born Tiny and Blind', it seems I was destined to have a fairly regular relationship with the media. But my first experience of television was at primary school.

An American television company came over to film at Jordanstown when I was about seven years old. They wanted to investigate how the children of Northern Ireland were being affected by the Troubles and what impact this might be having on their interaction and relationships. The TV company selected me and another girl, Bernadette, to be closely observed both at school and at home. We came from different sides of the divide — Bernadette was a Catholic and I was Protestant — but we were firm friends.

The experience of being filmed was fun for us at the time. The camera crew followed me while I was travelling home on the school bus and filmed me being dropped off at our house, by that time in East Belfast. Then they filmed me riding up and down the street on my bike, a two-wheeler which my grandfather had fitted with stabilisers. Then they filmed my grandmother talking about her views on the Troubles and her thoughts on the future. Granny, however, had something else on her mind, as I remember all too clearly. A few weeks before the cameras turned up to film, our house had been flooded when a pipe at the back of the washing machine had burst. All the carpet in the living room and stairs had had to be lifted and sent for cleaning, leaving the bare tiles exposed. My poor grandmother was worried about how this would look when the documentary was shown all over America.

I remember, too, the day the whole school gathered for the video of the end product. We couldn't have been more dismayed and confused. The film producer had twisted events to make it seem as though Bernadette and I argued with each other and fought about our different religious beliefs. Even though we were close friends, the documentary portrayed us as enemies. It was crazy – we were only seven years old. But that's the media for you. It did not seem to occur to them to show the positive side of Northern Ireland and highlight the fact that there were schools that were integrated and where religion was not an issue for the children. Perhaps it didn't suit their agenda. Young as I was, I was devastated. I never found out what Bernadette's family thought about it.

✳

When I was older, I started taking more of an interest in what was going on around me, in the politics and religion of Northern Ireland, and the Troubles became more of a talking point. I would question my Catholic friends about what they were taught in their religious education classes and I found the differences between the two strands of Christianity very interesting. Why were there different interpretations of the Bible, and how come the beliefs of Catholics and Protestants were so different?

There were frequent confrontations between Protestant and Catholic children about the rights and wrongs of what was happening, yet the differences never caused any problems between me and my friends and I didn't get involved in the arguments as it all seemed pointless to me. But I clearly recall one of my classmates coming into school complaining he felt sick and dizzy after being hit by a paint bomb the night before while rioting with the police in West Belfast. He would have been only about twelve years old and he was partially sighted. It seemed crazy that children as young as this and even younger – six and seven year olds – were allowed to get involved in that sort of behaviour; they still join in now if there are riots.

CHAPTER 2

Taunts and Treats

———✳———

Being blind was not a problem for me as I was growing up. It didn't seem to hold me back from doing the things I wanted to do as a child – I had a bicycle, a swing in the garden and my friends at school. But this didn't mean that life was entirely carefree or that I didn't have some hard lessons to learn about human nature.

My memories of Jordanstown School are fond ones, but my experience convinced me that it is better, where at all possible, for children with any form of disability to be educated in mainstream schools as this teaches able-bodied children about impairment and to accept disabled pupils. At Jordanstown, we weren't given the chance to mix with able-bodied children and so missed out on learning how to cope with the cruelty and ignorance of children who have no visible impairment. I know things have improved since then, with disabled children now being educated alongside able-bodied pupils, and I'm glad of it.

The only opportunity I had to mix with children outside school was in the street, and I can still remember the snide remarks and taunts I had to endure. The kids knew I couldn't react to their bullying by running after them or fighting back. Some of them would shout 'blind eyes' after me, which made sense however unkind it was, or 'four eyes', which showed that they didn't always think about what they were saying because I didn't wear glasses. They would come up and ask me how many fingers they were holding up, and when I couldn't answer they'd laugh at me – 'You can't tell me because you can't see.' I wouldn't cry in front of them; I saved my tears for when I got home.

Even though I was blind, it was a mystery to me why the children wouldn't ask me to play with them. I couldn't run about and chase but there were word games and other less frenetic activities that I would have loved to have joined in with. Now, of course, I know that theirs was a natural instinct to bully another child who was different, much as the herd or pack will turn on an animal that is weak or wounded.

Not all the children teased me though. I had a number of friends who accepted my disability and would protect me from the others. And the taunting eventually stopped – I would have been around eleven or twelve at this time – when I learned to turn the jibes around. If I was asked how many fingers my tormentor was holding up, I would say, 'I don't know, but why don't you tell me?' or 'I can't see how many fingers you have in front of me. How would you feel if you were in my position?' This made them stop and think. When they realised I wasn't letting their remarks get to me they became curious and asked me questions about my blindness – 'How do you read books?' 'How do you watch TV?' 'How can you see your food to eat it?' Once the kids saw that my disability was quite interesting, their attitude changed and I became quite popular.

However, there was one incident, when I was about ten, that took bullying to new and dangerous levels. I was running up the street one day, brushing my fingertips along the fences as I always did, when I tripped over a bicycle in front of me. The handlebar was pointing upwards and the brake handle went into my left eye. I made for home with what I thought were tears trickling down my face – I didn't realise it was blood.

One of my aunts laid me on the sofa and put a cloth over my eye, and then a neighbour took me to hospital. On the way, he told us he had seen a boy watching me come up the street and had seen him deliberately put the bike in front of me. According to the doctors, I was very lucky not to have lost my eyeball. (In fact, my left eye *is* artificial now; nothing to do with the bike incident, I had to have it replaced in 1999 when the eyeball became infected.) The boy was about two years older than me and his deliberate cruelty shocked the other kids in the street, who were really supportive. The culprit's mother on the other hand didn't bother to discipline him, excusing him on the grounds that he didn't understand what blindness was. A twelve year old?

This was one of the very few accidents I had while I was growing up – quite amazing under the circumstances. But then, as I was to discover, other forces were already at work on my behalf.

✳

Apart from the occasional taunts, life was good, and from the age of four and a half my childhood unfolded happily enough against the backdrop of school at Jordanstown, my grandparents and aunties, first in South and later in East Belfast, and those waymarks in the year that are such a highlight in the life of a child and so evocative later for the adult.

Easter was the first of these. It always brought a new outfit for me and lots of Easter eggs. If the weather was good my grandfather would take us all out for a picnic in his minibus. As well as paid trips – bus runs, Sunday school outings and so forth – he and his minibus did volunteer work for the parents of Muckamore Abbey, a hospital just outside Belfast for mentally disturbed children and adults. I used to love going for 'runs', as we called our outings. Sometimes we would go to the seaside or perhaps for a drive south to Dublin in the Republic. I can still remember the egg and onion sandwiches that Granny used to make for these trips and, if we were lucky, buns with icing and jam in them, and the mixing bowl to lick when she had finished with it.

Then there was 12 July, an important holiday for Protestants in Northern Ireland when they celebrate the Battle of the Boyne in 1690. This event is renowned for its Orange Order parades that take marchers and bands through different areas of the province in a carnival-like atmosphere. Although the parades were primarily aimed at the Protestant community many Catholics turned out to watch them too. And I had another new outfit for the occasion.

We always used to celebrate Halloween in style in Northern Ireland, and 31 October would find us putting candles in the lanterns we had made from hollowing out turnips and pumpkins. When it got dark we dressed up as witches, vampires and ghouls (false faces and all) and went out collecting round the neighbours, hoping for nuts, apples or sweets. Then back to the house we would go for the best part of the day – dumpling. This is a type of fruit loaf made from mixed fruit, spices and suet, which Granny would have prepared early the same morning. The smell of it wafted through the house for hours as it simmered away, before it was put beside the fire to dry out. Coins were hidden in the dumpling and we all searched, hoping to be the one to find them. Then we might play ducking for nuts, which involved putting our heads in a basin of water and trying to grab a nut between our teeth.

Halloween is still celebrated in Northern Ireland but not on such a big scale. Some people continue the tradition of putting out food offerings for the souls who are supposed to walk the earth on All Hallows' Eve, still believing that the house will be wrecked if there isn't an offering.

And Christmas, of course. This is surely *the* time of year, above all others, for children, and everyone will have memories of this magical festivity. I must be honest and say that I never celebrated Christmas from a religious perspective, though the family did. Even as a child, religion held no attraction for me. Certainly, I went to Sunday school, and indeed won prizes for attendance and answering questions – I remember being presented with the Gospel of St Luke in Braille. I even have an O level in Religious Education. But I was never drawn to believe and took hardly any of it on board.

Nevertheless, Christmas was a special time and my memories of it are vivid. Going to see Santa Claus was a hugely enjoyable treat, and I got the chance to meet him on several occasions: once with the pupils at Jordanstown, then with my family, and for several years at a party that was organised for disabled children by a community group in Belfast. I can still remember the song we had to sing there, 'Do you love old Santa Claus?', 'Yes, yes, yes we do!' we'd all shout. Then in came Santa Claus and we were led up to him for our gift. Like most youngsters, I used to ask him how he could be in so many places at the same time, and of course received the same answer from him as children all over the world:

'I'm magic'. At home, my stepfather Jim used to dress up as Santa on Christmas day and come over to Granny's house in the evening distributing presents with a 'Ho, ho, ho' – his voice always gave him away of course.

✳

I loved anything that engaged and stimulated my mind, so my favourite pastimes tended to be board games and listening to a cassette recorder or radio. I can remember in particular playing a game called Frustration, and it was certainly that. Frustration consisted of a hexagonal board with a plastic dome in the centre. This contained a dice, which you threw by pressing on the dome. Four sets of coloured pieces – green, red, yellow and blue – fitted into the holes on the board, and you moved these according to the number on the dice. The aim of the game was to try to knock your opponents' pieces off the board. As long as I had someone sighted to play with me, I could knock their pieces off the board for hours. Braille Scrabble and dominoes were other favourites.

One of the best things I remember getting as a child was a talking telephone. My mum had it sent to me from the United States. Telephones fascinated me, and I used to have imaginary conversations with all kinds of people. Similarly, listening to the transistor radio or to my cassette recorder kept me occupied for hours, especially as I got older, when I would take the radio with me on the bus to school so I could listen to it on the journey there and back.

But for some strange reason, a radio would usually last me only a year before its motor burnt out. It wasn't as if I left them on or overused them, but I managed to go through so many as I was growing up that my family got quite annoyed and used to blame me for breaking them. It was just as frustrating for me, but at the time we gave little thought as to why electrical appliances kept breaking down around me.

Most little girls have a doll and pram and love dressing up and putting on toy make-up. None of these activities appealed to me, except for a doctor's medical case and uniform I was given; it was the only thing I would dress up in. If I had been sighted I would definitely have gone into the medical profession. But as for the rest, I didn't have much use for them. Not being sighted, I couldn't imitate how someone might care for a baby, and I didn't know how to apply make-up. I still don't wear it today, not because I'm blind – many blind people are taught how to apply make-up – but because I'm concerned that cosmetics can damage one's skin. I don't really see the point of it either, and feel much the same way about dyeing or perming my hair. There are a few grey streaks in mine now and my friends have suggested highlights, but I don't believe we should tamper with the natural process of ageing. Sighted people worry too much about how they look and not enough about the fact that it's personality, what's inside, that really counts.

＊

So, no doll and pram for me. I have held many babies in my time but I have to admit that I never had the maternal instinct myself, though I was surrounded by youngsters when I was a child. Our little house in East Belfast was always full, and not just with members of our family. Granny fostered Chinese children whose parents had to work in their restaurants and couldn't look after them. They would sometimes call her 'mummy' but she would explain that she wasn't their mother and always insist on them calling her 'granny'. It was heart-breaking for us when the kids had to go home to their families.

Taking me on must have been a huge responsibility for Granny. I needed much more attention than most children, both because of my blindness and because, as a toddler, I was constantly ill with chest infections and pneumonia. She would have had to teach me all the things that sighted children pick up from watching their parents and siblings, such as dressing, tying shoelaces and using cutlery. Toilet training would have been especially difficult for me to learn; I wouldn't have been able to see other kids using a potty or known what it was for.

As for me, my first few years were confusing and disorientating in so many ways. The frequent visits to hospital, learning to do by touch the things that sighted kids took for granted. And in the middle of everything else, there were the nightmares.

CHAPTER 3

First Signs

——✳——

The nightmares started when I was about five years old. I can remember them as if it were yesterday. They came without warning, perhaps once a fortnight or so, but it was always the same dream and followed the same pattern. I would wake up suddenly with sweat pouring from me, paralysed with fear, because I could hear voices but did not know who they belonged to. It was as if people were talking quietly in my room – and I knew the voices were talking to me. I would strain with all my might to catch what they were saying, but the words were scrambled and confused. Sometimes they sounded like the burblings of an adult trying to talk to a baby; at other times, it was like listening to a radio that wasn't tuned in properly. It was an awful experience for such a young child. The voices would stop when I became hysterical and, terrified, ran downstairs into the living room screaming to my grandmother, 'They're back, the voices, they're back.'

'Who are they, Sharon? What are they saying?' My granny would try to get some sense out of me.

'I don't know. I can't understand them,' I'd sob. 'It feels like there's something over my mouth and I can't talk.'

I was inconsolable. Nothing she or anyone else could say would soothe my fears, so Granny would ring up Mr Hare, who had healed me when I was younger. As he spoke to me over the phone, I would calm down. It always worked.

Unable to predict when the nightmares would disturb my sleep and the voices might pay me a visit, I would dread going to bed. Back then, I had no idea who the voices belonged to or whether they were male or female; I was always too frightened to register any of these details.

The sensation of having something placed over my mouth and of not being able to talk, brought with it the strangest feeling that I wasn't allowed to discuss with anybody else what the voices were telling me. This was more of an intuition on my part than an overt instruction from whoever was trying to communicate with me. In hindsight, I know the unseen visitors were not in any way aggressive. The fear arose from my inability to understand why they were coming to me and what they were trying to tell me. Why did they come at night and not during the day? No one else had visitors in the night, did they?

What made my distress worse was the absence of any physical impression of my visitors. Would I have been able to see them if I had been sighted, I wondered. It wasn't until I got older that I discovered the answers to these questions.

My family couldn't get to the bottom of the nightmares and concluded that they must be something to do with my travelling to and from school with deaf children. They assumed that I was frightened of the sounds that deaf people often make without realising that they are doing it, and that this fear presented in my dreams. I knew this wasn't the case.

The nightmare episodes stopped for a year when I was six, and I was at last able to sleep in peace. However, the unseen visitors hadn't given up trying to make their presence felt; they simply changed tactics.

Something altogether new and startling began to happen to me when I turned seven. Unusually for a blind person, I had always dreamed in images and in colour. Now, images started miraculously to appear in my head when I was awake. My unseen visitors were connecting with me during the day.

Pictures were projected on to my mind as if it were a screen – I could see them just as if I had been sighted. They would usually be of an object and, at the same time as seeing this in my mind's eye, I might also experience the sensation of touching it. Sometimes the image was a written message – as if printed on a page, the letters clearly recognisable even though I had only ever experienced Braille and raised print.

This time I wasn't too frightened. There were no strange visitors in the night, just these intriguing images. Even though I was still very young and had no understanding of what was going on and no knowledge of the paranormal, I did make the connection between these images and my dream visitors. The new development excited and scared me a little at the same time. Above all, I was curious, though I still assumed the experience was normal, that everyone had these images and sensations.

The images were never to do with me; I never saw my clothes or my personal belongings for example; they would always relate to something external, something going on around me or at school. One day we were having a lesson on the skeletal system of the body. The teacher was explaining to us that we had to have a framework of bones in our body otherwise we would collapse like jellies. There was a plastic model of the skeleton for us to touch so that we could get a sensory impression of what she was describing.

Before I could touch the skeleton, a picture flashed into my mind of what it would be like. If I had been sighted I would most likely have seen a picture of a skeleton by then, but I simply had no idea of what one looked like – yet there it was in my mind.

At school we used to listen to BBC television's *Near and Far* education programmes. The series reconstructed historical events and as the programme discussed, say, new inventions, I now began to get simultaneous pictures in my mind of what was happening on the screen. I could 'see' this happening and my images matched the commentary.

Looking back, it seems strange that I didn't ask any of my classmates if they had ever experienced the same kind of thing. But back then I thought this was normal. Everyone had pictures in their mind, didn't they?

The mind images continued to come to me at random. They lasted only a few seconds at first, but if I focused on them I could hold the picture in my head a little longer.

About this time, I became aware that I had another talent. Again I thought it was perfectly normal. Nature studies was one of the subjects on the curriculum at Jordanstown, and the teacher would take us into the school grounds for nature walks so we could learn about the natural world – flowers, trees, fruit and vegetables. We would explore the trees with our hands and pick bluebells, but I now realise that I gleaned a good deal more than my classmates on these expeditions.

When I touched a tree, it felt warm to my fingers, no matter what the ambient temperature – I could feel the energy coming from it. I learned to tell the difference between one tree and another from the temperature of the energy it gave off. An oak would feel warm to the touch but have a strong pulsing sensation emanating in waves up and down the trunk. A horse chestnut's energy would be cooler and the pulse weaker and slower.

When I examined a bluebell gently with my fingertips, the warmth it gave off was not the same as that of a rose, it had a lighter energy. And when the flowers were picked, I experienced a sense of sadness; I fancied that if the flowers could speak they would have screamed. These observations seemed as normal to me as breathing; it was after all what we were on the nature walk to learn, so I never discussed my discoveries with the teacher or my friends.

The emotional aspect of this strange sensitivity came over me more powerfully the first time I was taken to the zoo. I could feel the frustration of the caged animals. I was there in the cage experiencing the loathing of being confined behind bars and not being able to tell anyone how I felt. I am not Dr Doolittle and I can't talk to animals – I was simply tuning into their auras.

Everything is made up of energy. We know there are different forms of it: electrical, thermal, mechanical, nuclear, for example. There is another type of energy called electromagnetism, commonly known as the aura. Everything has an aura – humans, animals, minerals and plants; its presence has been scientifically proven by infrared photography developed by Semyon Kirlian in Russia. This was the energy I was picking up from the trees and flowers even though at the age of seven I knew nothing of energy and auras.

✳

My unseen visitors had started to come to me again as I slept, but this time their voices did not seem as frightening as before, and now my dreams were of an entirely different nature.

Blind people, as I've mentioned, are not generally thought to dream in images since, without any visual references, the brain is not able to translate data into pictures. It would be like downloading a file into a computer without the software to translate it. When sighted people dream they use all five senses in the same way as they would in the waking state. When blind people dream their four functioning senses come to the fore – sound, smell, taste and touch – but not sight.

My dreams were different. I was taken to beautiful places where all my senses were awakened. I would find myself standing in an incredible wonderland, surrounded by the sounds of nature. Running water from streams, fountains or waterfalls blended with bird song and the buzzing of insects. Yet it wasn't just the sounds that made these places special for me. It was the fact that I could see. I could actually see the short, velvety, green grass I was standing on, and the rolling hills and trees around me.

At first, I was completely unnerved by what was happening. How could I visualise grass as well as touch it? How could I walk around this place without being guided by someone? Why didn't I have this freedom during the day?

When I woke from these episodes, I felt wonderfully calm and relaxed but frustrated. I wanted to stay there. I felt more awake in my dreams than I did in reality, so why could I only see at night while I slept and not during the day when I was awake?

Was I imagining this wonderland? All children have a secret place they visit in their fantasies, but how can you conjure up an imaginary world if you've never seen the real world, never seen colours, a stream, a landscape? I was to discover that I could not only see colours in my dreams but I would be able to 'see' them when awake too.

When I was ten years old two doctors came to the school from Russia to research the possibility that blind children could identify primary colours by touch. I was among the pupils who were selected for the experiment. We were excused from some lessons, and the school allocated the doctors an empty Portakabin so we wouldn't be distracted by outside influences. The doctors make us lie on sleeping bags on the floor and relax by taking deep breaths and releasing our muscles. We loved it. Not only was the experiment great fun and a diversion from lessons, it was a novelty. About half a dozen of us took part, and while I don't know how the selection process was arrived at or who selected us, I do know that those who were chosen had never experienced any degree of sight; we were all blind from birth, in contrast to some of the other pupils at Jordanstown who were partially sighted or had lost their sight when very young.

After the relaxation session, each of us had to come up in turn to a desk and hold our hands over pieces of material. These were of different textures and compositions — cardboard, felt, paper, sandpaper and so on. With our hands raised a few inches above a sample, we had to try to work out what colour it was by feeling the temperature it gave off. One of the doctors replaced the piece with a different sample of another colour for us to analyse, while the other observed and made notes.

Every colour has a unique temperature. It is no myth that blue is a cold colour and red is hot. With practice, I learned to distinguish between the hot and cold colours and the ones that were neither, such as yellow or green. They felt cooler than red but not as cold as blue. It didn't matter which texture of material we were given, the results were the same. Some days I got better results than others, but this depended on whether I was concentrating or not.

Over the sessions the number of pupils was reduced. Eventually, there were only two of us left, myself and another girl. It seemed we were getting results far above what could be explained by mere chance. We never found out what the doctors were planning to do with the findings of the research and, sadly, after they left the school to return to Russia we never heard any more about their project and their findings.

However, the experiment with colours marked another stage for me. In addition to the images flashed into my mind, I began to get a heightened sense of the unseen visitors who invaded my dreams. It was as if they had been waiting for the opportunity to step up their campaign to attract my attention, to let me know that they hadn't given up trying to communicate directly with me. Their communication with me was very subtle at first – clearly my visitors didn't want to frighten me as they had initially done in the nightmares of five years before – but gradually I started to hear their voices during the day, and their approach was more child friendly this time. To begin with, the voices helped me with comparatively small things. I was doing a geography essay on the Masai people of Kenya and my unseen visitors gave me details and key words that weren't in the textbook: the Masai ate yams, not potatoes; yams were spelled 'y a m s'.

While I was writing an essay on the circulation of the blood, the voices pointed out that I had made a mistake: 'the veins bring blood *back* to the heart'. Just a light steer, but to a child of ten at school this was the kind of thing that mattered.

There is little doubt in my mind now that the experiment with the Russian doctors had acted as a catalyst, activating certain special abilities. Again, I had been introduced to the right people at the right time.

CHAPTER 4

Strange Happenings

——*——

The step up to secondary school is an exciting turning point in the life of most children, but the transition did not hold any particular thrills for us at Jordanstown. We didn't have to sit the 'eleven plus' or go to a new school, we simply moved from the primary part of Jordanstown to the secondary, and the only difference was a fuller, more structured timetable, different subjects and teachers and, naturally, much more homework. I enjoyed most of the classes, though my least favourite subject was, and still is, mathematics. I have never been any good at figures, unfortunately, and I used to dread these lessons.

The voices didn't always come to my aid when I needed them. They tended to help me out with those subjects that I was most interested in, such as geography, biology or science. Perhaps they realised helping me in maths was a waste of their time.

Home economics was another subject I hated. Living alone as I do these days, I have no choice but to cook for myself, though I often cheat and buy ready-made meals that can go straight into the oven. At Jordanstown, however, home economics was important and involved learning a lot of new skills. We had to be taught far more than sighted children, not just how to mix ingredients, for example, but how to tell by touch when the mixture had reached the right consistency. Sighted people can see when food is ready but we had to learn to judge this by other means. Although there are many devices to help blind people in the kitchen, such as Braille measuring jugs and Braille temperature marks on the oven, simple tasks like lifting burning hot containers out of the oven and carrying them to the work surface without spilling the contents require a certain technique. This might involve rehearsing first with casseroles filled with water to make sure we were holding them at the correct angle and knew where the lip of the pot was. All this had to be learned.

I must admit that I wasn't always as attentive as I should have been during some lessons, and this was particularly true of my English classes, which I regret now. The English teacher was a Mr Anderson; he was completely blind which, of course, made it was easier for the pupils to get away with more in his classes, and we took every opportunity to mess around. It was wrong and I certainly wouldn't have liked being treated so badly, but when you're twelve years old, other people's feelings, especially those of teachers, aren't very high on your agenda. (I should say at this point that I have since grown to love English and even re-sat my English O level later at college and got a grade B.)

One day during an English lesson with Mr Anderson something rather odd happened. He had to leave the classroom for a few moments, and told us to get on with our reading while he was away. The class, of course, had other ideas. For once, I did as instructed and concentrated on the reading, so wasn't involved in the ensuing rumpus.

When Mr Anderson returned to the room he demanded to know who had been causing the disruption. As usual, nobody owned up, so he said we would all have to be punished. This involved lining up in front of him and giving him a hand to be slapped with a ruler. Mr Anderson wasn't moved by my pleas that I hadn't done anything wrong and I had to join the queue. I turned to a friend and whispered furiously, 'This isn't going to happen. I'm not getting slapped for something I haven't done.' Without knowing why, I focused my mind on the plastic ruler in the teacher's hand and imagined it breaking in half when it came to my turn.

I approached Mr Anderson reluctantly and held out my hand. There was a loud crack, and one half of the ruler flew across the room. I stood frozen with panic and fear. Nothing quite like this had happened to me before. How could the ruler have broken? Surely it couldn't have had anything to do with me, or could it?

Mr Anderson passed it off as a joke, saying that obviously rulers weren't supposed to be used for slapping people. And everyone else laughed and said what a pity the ruler hadn't broken *before* he'd had the chance to use it. But I knew that something out of the ordinary had taken place and that perhaps it wasn't some-thing to laugh about.

This incident, it soon turned out, wasn't just a one-off. I was going to have to learn to curb my temper. One day I went into the girls' changing rooms between classes for a drink of water from the drinking fountain. A group of deaf girls were changing for PE and one of them, probably mistaking me for a partially sighted pupil, grabbed me and tried to push me out of the room back into the corridor. I didn't like the girl pushing me around and, once again, anger welled up inside me. I concentrated hard on the door closing. It seemed to move of its own accord, and suddenly I found myself in the corridor, my adversary in the changing room and the door between us shut fast.

Thankfully these strange incidents were few and far between, but I realised things could get out of hand. Not knowing what had caused them was the worst thing. No voices or images came into my head in these moments of high emotion; the results seemed to be produced entirely from within myself.

A film that was very popular at the time (and still is) gave me cause for thought. *Carrie* portrays the same kind of phenomena that I had experienced, though of course being a horror movie it exaggerated them for effect. Still, it made me wary and I became very careful to control my temper at school.

Since then there has been the occasional loss of control when something similar has happened, usually involving light bulbs shattering and kettles blowing up. Once, when I was still living with my aunts, I had come back from shopping with my cousin Elizabeth and was standing in the kitchen while the kettle boiled for a cup of tea.

'What have you been buying, Sharon?' Aunt Roberta asked. 'You've been spending your money on CDs again, haven't you? Why are you always buying more? Haven't you got enough of them?'

This was quite unfair. For once, I hadn't added to my CD collection, and I didn't see why I should be interrogated about my shopping trip anyway. I started to get angry.

Suddenly, there was a hiss of steam and a crack. The smell of burning plastic and rubber filled the room, the kettle blew into smithereens and water went everywhere. Luckily, no one was scalded and, not knowing anything about the incidents at school, my family didn't suspect that the exploding kettle had anything to do with me, least of all that I could inadvertently influence events if I lost my temper.

But the kettle incident brought me up short – I hadn't been concentrating on it or anything else for that matter. These days I know better. When I am involved in a confrontation I will try to walk away or at least keep calm.

Despite the fact that I now feel in complete control of my energy, people have remarked that the lights in my apartment will dim when I am arguing a point passionately. Electrical appliances continue to act strangely around me, much as years ago my transistor radios burnt out. Light bulbs blow; televisions switch themselves on and off; kettles boil of their own accord. When I'm in a radio studio, microphones, computers and lights suddenly turn off or shut down; and when I've been filming, video cameras will suddenly drain of power.

All this I now know is caused by electromagnetic energy, which interferes with electrical appliances. But I knew nothing of this when I was a child. I simply believed, as I did of my other sensory abilities, that everyone shared them. It was far too frightening to think otherwise – that I might be different, a freak. I believed that as long as I didn't lose my temper there wouldn't be a problem.

✳

So far my unseen visitors seemed to be happy to communicate with me over fairly small matters even though they were very important to me at the time. And they certainly made themselves useful.

At the end of the school year we had exams, which we all dreaded. We didn't like having to revise either, but it had to be done, and as I loved reading, revision turned out to be easier than I had expected. I only had to read something through once or twice before I could remember whole sections of a book, a very tidy skill when it came to revision. On the other hand, with subjects I didn't like, I would lose concentration.

This is when my unseen visitors would step in to give me a helping hand. The questions in certain test papers seemed remarkably familiar, as if I had seen them before – except that I hadn't. At other times, answers simply popped into my head. There was a difference between my memory coming up with an answer and being given the information by the unseen visitors. The voices would give me a keyword or sentence, which would bring the answer springing to mind. My memory, on the other hand, would recall phrases or sentences from the textbooks or notes.

At times like these I was glad of the help of my voices. I still didn't know who they belonged to or how many of them there were. I never attempted a conversation with any of them, and I suppose I just got into the habit of taking them for granted, especially as they were still only communicating with me regarding relatively insignificant matters. I certainly didn't work as hard as I could have done at Jordanstown – perhaps I didn't feel I had to.

Gradually, however, my unseen visitors started to make their presence felt in a more pronounced way. I'm not sure why this was and can only guess that being older, I was more aware of them and receptive to what they were trying to tell me. At any rate, their communication began to take a rather unexpected turn.

Throughout my years at school, my friends felt that I was someone they could talk to about their problems. Pupils who needed a friendly ear or advice often came to me, and the staff asked me to look after new kids who found it hard to fit into the routine or were bullied by others. How I hated bullying!

One such pupil was a girl named Heather, who came to Jordanstown from England. She was partially sighted and she also had mild epilepsy. The other children made fun of her accent and teased her about the epilepsy, accusing her of putting the fits on to avoid lessons.

The two of us were in the changing rooms one day getting ready for PE when suddenly I heard a voice in my mind warning that Heather was about to have a seizure. Then a dizziness came over me and I felt cold and unfocused.

Heather hadn't said anything to me, and it would have seemed very odd to ask her in detail, and in front of everyone, about how she was feeling; more importantly, I didn't want to draw attention to her as I knew the seizures embarrassed her. I waited until we were warming up outside on the hockey pitch before asking her quietly if she was all right. She insisted she was.

'Trust yourself, Sharon. Wait and see what happens,' said a voice in my head.

Just before the end of the lesson Heather went into a seizure. Later, I asked her to describe the sensations she experienced immediately before the fit. They were exactly what I had felt earlier in the changing room. The voice had been right.

I didn't say anything about this to Heather, and even though the voices were beginning to come through to me more often, I kept it to myself. I couldn't see the point in discussing with anyone something I didn't understand myself, and I was still fairly sure that there wasn't anything too remarkable about my voices. I pushed the matter to the back of my mind.

There were times when I made observations to my school friends about their moods or feelings, as if I were an aerial tuned into them. They would laugh and say I was having one of my 'spooky moments' but, thankfully, they seemed to think it was normal, so why shouldn't I?

*

As it was, my life was happy and full. Apart from school and homework, I had joined the Girl Guides. This was great fun and really challenging because I was the only blind member of our group. We learned team-building skills and went on sponsored walks, barbecues and camping trips. And it was with the Guides that I was introduced to first-aid skills. I had always been interested in anything medical and this was right up my street. To get my first-aid badge I had to take a course with the local Red Cross. Here I was not just the only totally blind member in the group, but in the whole of the Northern Ireland Red Cross. I loved the course and passed the exam with flying colours.

After that I left the Guides and joined the Red Cross. It was brilliant to go on duty with them to concerts, sporting events such as the Belfast Marathon, and, of course, the parades. At first, our group leader was reluctant to let me go on duty, but I protested, arguing that I had passed my exams under the same conditions as everyone else and that they should give me a chance. Obviously, there were some things I couldn't do, but I wanted to be as involved as everyone else, so I was allowed to wear the uniform and have my own first-aid kit.

The public reacted positively to me while on duty, and when we had to deal with anyone who had had a few drinks, I wasn't usually abused quite so roundly as other members of the team.

Sometimes I would know what was wrong with a casualty before I'd asked them. I was on duty at a parade one day when a man approached saying he had hurt his finger.

'Yes, his finger's fractured actually,' I said to my colleagues. In my mind I could see the break, though I couldn't tell the rest of the team exactly how I knew. I would have been able to diagnose the problem by touch anyway, since my touch is more sensitive because of reading Braille and having to use my hands as my eyes all the time. In the event, my diagnosis was correct.

On another occasion, I was on duty at a festival when we were called to attend to a woman who had apparently suffered an epileptic seizure. Her symptoms certainly matched this diagnosis, but a voice told me that she was suffering from an allergic reaction to something she had ingested. This was confirmed by the doctors when we got her to the hospital. She had recently been put on new medication and this is what had triggered the reaction.

And yet, I still didn't question too deeply how I was coming by all this information. It wasn't until the 1980s, when I went to England to a college for the blind, that I discovered what lay behind these insights and learned that my premonitions, images of injuries and ability to tune into other people's feelings were by no means normal.

CHAPTER 5

Life Changes

———✳———

In August 1979 something happened that was to change my life dramatically. My granny died. She had been ill on and off for years, and although the hospital had been unable to come up with a diagnosis and her consultant had insisted her heart was as strong as a bull's, it turned out that she had been suffering from congestive heart failure for some time. This problem wasn't diagnosed correctly until she went to another hospital; they kept her in for routine tests but she never came out. She died of heart failure. She was only in her late 50s.

I was staying with my mother at the time as my aunts were away. Assured by the doctors that Granny would be fine, they had flown off to Majorca on holiday.

When I visited Granny in hospital, she was drowsy and confused because, so they told us, she was on oxygen. It was disturbing to find her in this state. Granny had been perfectly coherent when she went into hospital. Now she couldn't hold a conversation and I'm not even sure she recognised my mother and me. This wasn't the warm, kind woman I remembered; she couldn't understand what was being said, but I sat and chatted to her as if everything were normal. While Mum was outside the ward speaking to the doctor, Granny kept asking me to lift her up. I thought she wanted to be lifted up in bed and together with a woman visiting another patient nearby we helped her into a sitting position. But Granny kept on asking to be lifted. Looking back now, I think she wanted to be released from her physical body.

The following day my mother went back to the hospital with my grandfather, while I stayed behind with my older brother. They returned home with news I had somehow never expected to hear.

'Sharon, Granny's dead,' Mum told me.

'No, she's not,' I sobbed unbelievingly. 'What's going to happen to me?'

I was fourteen. I had always lived with my grandmother, grandfather and the three aunts. Was all that about to change now my granny was gone? My head span and I felt cold and clammy. I was in shock. My aunts cut short their holiday and hurried home; they were just as devastated.

My granny, their mother, had always been there for us, the warm, solid presence at the centre of our household. How could she have been taken from us so suddenly and so early? She had only gone into hospital for routine tests. I was completely crushed by the thought that I would never hear her reassuring voice again, or be welcomed home from school with soda bread, helped with my homework or treated to her delicious muffins and cheese.

The day Granny's body was brought into the family home, my mother took me over to the coffin and asked if I wanted to touch her face and hair or kiss her goodbye. I had never touched a dead body before and was very reluctant, yet I knew that in order to move on I had to force myself to do it. Only by touching her would I finally be able to accept she was gone. I ran my fingers over her face, feeling her features for the last time, wanting to make sure I remembered what she looked like. It was still the kind face I knew so well, but now as cold as marble.

The night before the funeral I stayed with our next-door neighbours to make room for other relatives. I couldn't face going outside while they took my granny away, so I remained indoors listening in horror to the outpouring of grief coming from our house. I was too upset about losing her to go to the funeral, and the rest of the day passed in a haze of sorrow.

Sooner or later, however, decisions had to be made about my future, and a few days after the funeral my mother presented me with two choices: I could go home with her or I could stay with my aunts and my grandfather. I didn't hesitate. Granny's home, and my grandpa and aunts were familiar, I had always been with them and I had an established routine. I didn't want my life to change, and I knew my grandpa would want me to be there. So I decided to stay with them. But it took us a long time to get over my grandmother's death and for our lives to get back to any kind of normality.

One of my aunts was especially affected by Granny's death and tried twice to commit suicide in an attempt to join her mother. It was then that another of my aunts, Hettie, persuaded her to go to the spiritualist church, the only one of its kind in Northern Ireland.

This was a turning point for my aunt. At the church she received a message from a little girl who had died a long time before and was buried in the same grave as Granny. The girl explained that Granny couldn't come through herself as it was too soon after her death; she was resting on the spirit side and my aunt was to stop grieving because her mother was happy and watching over us. The medium gave other information about my grandmother that proved to my aunt that the communication was genuine and which the medium, who wasn't local but visiting from England, couldn't possibly have known otherwise.

My aunt drew real comfort from this experience; it opened her mind to the possibility that those who have died continue to live on in the spirit world and to the notion that there are spirits all around us. At the time I knew nothing about all this, or about survival evidence, as it is called. It was only later, when I started my own investigations into spiritualism, that I discovered my aunt had been to a spiritualist church and received a message about Granny.

✳

I thought that I had got over my feelings of grief at my grandmother's death years ago, but I don't think the loss of a loved one ever goes away. The pain of knowing you will never again hear their dear voice when you need their words of advice or comfort is always in your heart.

People think mediums do not have to suffer from such emotions because we can communicate with our loved ones, but they are mistaken. In fact, loss is often harder for a medium to bear. Although I know I could talk to my grandmother at any time, to this day I choose not to. Communicating with those who have passed on is not the same as talking to our loved ones face to face. Mediums don't receive a physical presence and it's this presence that we miss in the same way as anybody else who is grieving.

Having said that, my grandmother does pass messages to me

through intermediaries on the spirit side, and she also appears to me in dreams or when I am very relaxed. It has to be this way: if I were to talk to her directly, in the way I talk to others who have passed on, I would be overwhelmed by my own emotions, as people often are when their loved ones communicate with them through a medium. Although I spend my life helping to ease the pain of others who have to cope with loss, I am human too. I feel the same sense of loss today that I did as a fourteen-year-old on the day I was told she had died.

✻

It seems to me now that my life was always destined to be a series of groundbreaking experiences, another of which was looming on my horizon. I was the first girl from Northern Ireland to be accepted at Hethersett in England, a further education college in Reigate, Surrey that specialised in preparing blind and visually impaired youngsters for independent living.

Granny had always been very protective of me, and I knew there was no way she would have allowed me to go to Hethersett if she had been alive. My grandfather, too, was unhappy about letting me go to England, but my aunts said that if it was what I wanted they wouldn't stand in my way. After all, it wasn't that far away and I would be home for holidays.

Two of the aunts travelled with me to Reigate to meet the Hethersett staff and look around the college. It seemed a nice place and the staff were friendly; they assured me that if I didn't settle in I was free to go home at any time. This was the first new school I had been to since primary, and the idea filled me with excitement.

Granny had been so protective that she hadn't let me do anything around the house. But being a typical teenager, tidying up and washing dishes wasn't high on my list of priorities, so not being allowed to do them wasn't too much of a sacrifice. To be honest, I could have made a bigger effort and offered to help more often, but I shamelessly accepted the disability card. Hethersett would make up for my lack of education in this department. It offered not only an academic curriculum but the opportunity to learn other essential life skills. The college put great emphasis on encouraging us to live as independently as possible. We would learn how to wash, iron and fold clothes properly, how to make beds, how to carry out small maintenance jobs such as wiring a plug and changing a fuse and a light bulb, and how to use buses and trains.

Sighted children learn these skills by watching their parents, but blind children have to be taught. There are so many things sighted people take for granted. Take traffic lights for instance. Once, while I was in London for a weekend with my Aunt Mavis and Uncle Terry, Mavis had pointed out that the green man was flashing. I asked her where he was, why he was green and why he was flashing in the middle of a London street. She laughed, explaining that the green man was a signal that let pedestrians know when to cross the road.

＊

At the end of June 1980, when I was almost fifteen, I left Jordanstown School ready to start at Hethersett that September. This was to be another milestone in my life, not just academically but in my psychic development. Once again, I was in the right place at the right time and met someone who would change the course of my life in a big way.

Arriving at Hethersett, I was nervous and confused despite the excitement. I had never been separated from my family, which was difficult enough, but I had never been in a boarding school before either. There was a whole new etiquette to learn. Everything was signalled by a hand bell in the hall which the staff or students rang at appointed times such as meals.

I shared a three-bed dormitory with two girls, and communal bathrooms and toilets with the other girls on the floor. The first challenge was to keep my things tidy in a confined space – we only had a cupboard each for our personal belongings.

I can remember my first night in the dormitory vividly. The other girls had been at boarding school together and talked between themselves. One of them was totally blind like me and the other partially sighted, but when I tried to make conversation they would answer curtly and carry on talking to each other. I was to find out why the following day.

At breakfast I made attempts to get to know the other students at my table but got the same cold shoulder treatment as the girls had given me in the dorm the night before. At first I put it down to communication problems: there were students at Hethersett from all over the country and I had difficulty understanding some of them. Perhaps, I thought, they couldn't make out my Belfast accent. But it wasn't my accent. I was the first student from Belfast, and as far as the other students were concerned, I was a terrorist. I couldn't believe it.

But, being only sixteen and having lived a relatively sheltered life, I didn't realise then how much discrimination existed in England towards people from Northern Ireland in the 1980s because of the bombings on the mainland. Of course, neither I nor my family had anything to do with this, it was simply guilt by association, and by some extraordinary leap of the imagination the students seemed to think that I might be carrying a gun or something.

The staff, on the other hand, were very supportive, and after a while a single bedroom made life easier for me.

I was determined not to allow prejudice to stand in my way. I wasn't at Hethersett to socialise but to learn, and I wasn't giving up that easily. Only once did my resolution waver, almost giving way to the temptation to call my family and ask them to arrange a flight back to Belfast, but the staff member on duty talked me out of it. He reassured me that things would settle down – and he was right.

Life carried on that first half of the term, and I buried myself in the work. I was delighted to find the classes both interesting and informative. We studied English, Braille, shorthand, telephony and typing among many other things, all of which would turn out to be useful skills in later years.

Occasionally, there were reminders of my Belfast roots. One day, during an English lesson, a siren blared out. It sounded just like the bomb siren at Jordanstown, and I knew exactly what I had to do. I got up, walked to the classroom door and waited to be taken out to the playground by the teacher. We had been drilled to do this in Belfast until it was instinctive. Not for a moment did I stop to think that I was in a different country or classroom.

'What are you doing?' the astonished teacher asked. It was the English accent that brought me back to earth with a shock.

My face burned with embarrassment as I went back to my desk. 'I thought that was the bomb siren,' I muttered.

'You're not in Northern Ireland now,' the teacher laughed. 'That's the Thames siren. It warns that the barrier is being raised during high tides.' I was expecting the other students to laugh too, but they didn't. So I explained about the bomb siren drills that we had been taught at school, and how when you went into town you stood at the entrance to the stores waiting for the security people to search your handbag and scan you with the metal detector for guns or explosives. This was standard procedure in Northern Ireland at that time. There was a total and embarrassed silence. I don't think the other students had the remotest idea what life was like in Northern Ireland.

They finally started to accept me after the first half term, and to my relief I began to fit in and make friends. I never told my family about the treatment I'd received when I first arrived because they might have insisted I come home. I hate having to ask for help because I always prefer to handle any problems that crop up myself, and I usually manage, but there was one occasion at Hethersett when I had to ask my mother to step in.

It was winter and the snow was quite deep. I had been feeling ill with a cold; sweat was pouring from me, I felt dizzy and I couldn't keep any food down. The matron wasn't in the surgery and the college housekeeper was standing in for her. When I described my symptoms she put her hand on my forehead, then accused me of trying to get out of lessons. This really upset me. I had never reported sick without reason, even at Jordanstown, and I knew I should be in bed. That night I rang my mother and explained the situation. She rang the headmaster at home and the next morning I was called into the surgery to be examined by a doctor. It turned out I had gastric flu. A few days in bed with the correct medication put me back on my feet and, curiously, the vindication boosted my confidence. Even if I had had to seek help from Mum, it had been my decision to take matters into my own hands, and it gave me a satisfied feeling.

I knew moving away from home and from Belfast would be hard, but my first term at Hethersett had thrown up an entirely unexpected set of obstacles. In addition to all the subjects I had looked forward to learning in England were some hard lessons in human nature. I had been placed in very much the same position as the friend of mine, Heather, in Belfast who had come to Jordanstown from England. Now I knew how she had felt and was glad that I'd helped her to cope with it.

January 1981 came around very quickly. I had returned to Belfast for the Christmas holiday, and it was time to go back to Hethersett for the new term. This time I was really looking forward to it. On my return, I found that in addition to the usual curriculum we were being offered the opportunity of taking a yoga course one evening a week. I was already doing judo for the sports section of my Duke of Edinburgh Bronze Award and, as I thought yoga was some kind of martial art, I eagerly signed up to the class.

I soon discovered that yoga was actually a very gentle method of using certain postures to relax the mind and body. This didn't put me off; quite the contrary in fact. I loved these classes and, being double jointed, I could get into most of the positions with ease. But it was the beginning of the class that was best of all.

The teacher, Valerie, would start off by asking us to lie on sleeping bags and let our minds and bodies relax, lulling us with a soothing voice, and soon I was far away from the gym, by a stream in a forest or on a beach. There were times during these classes when I felt as if I were being taken back to the place of my childhood dreams and would feel the same sense of frustration when the teacher brought me back to reality and my physical surroundings.

I had been going to yoga for about six weeks when Valerie asked if she could have a word in private at the end of the lesson. Puzzled, I stayed behind to find out what she wanted. I was about to have one of the most important conversations of my life.

'So, how do you like the yoga lessons?' she asked.

I was enthusiastic, explaining that I was doing judo as well and that the yoga classes were really good for my posture, that the relaxation was boosting my concentration and that the exercises were keeping me supple.

'Glad to hear you're enjoying it. You're a natural,' she said.

Her next words threw me into a state of confusion. 'So, how long have you been practising?' she asked casually.

'I've never done yoga before,' I said, delighted she thought I was so fit.

'No,' she came back. 'Not yoga. I mean how long have you been a medium?'

I still didn't understand what she was on about. 'I'm not a medium, I'm a size ten,' I insisted.

'I'm not talking about your clothes,' she laughed. 'I'm talking about your gift.'

CHAPTER 6

Proof Positive

————✻————

I left the gym that day with my mind in a whirl. With her customary calm, Valerie had gone on to say that she thought I could be psychic, that I might have the gift of mediumship. Psychic? Medium? I didn't have a clue what she was talking about and had told her so.

Unruffled, she explained that although she didn't have these gifts herself, she could read my aura and recognised them in me. 'You will find out in time, Sharon. Things will happen and you will be drawn to look closer at what I'm talking about.'

I rushed back to the college library to consult the encyclopedia, the talking version of *Encyclopedia Britannica*, indexed in Braille. I looked up 'psychic', 'medium' and 'aura'. According to *Britannica*, mediums were able to receive information from souls who had passed on, without using the five known senses. Psychics could tap into information about past, present and future events using one of three methods: clairvoyance, the ability to see clearly without physical sight; clairaudience, the ability to hear without physical hearing; and clairsentience, the ability to feel without touch. The aura was an electromagnetic energy that surrounded all living matter and consisted of different colours that resonated with the chakras (or energy centres) of the body.

All this was very interesting, but it didn't seem to have any relevance to me. I couldn't do any of this stuff. I couldn't talk to dead people. Abandoning *Britannica*, I felt vaguely disappointed. I had hoped so fervently that it might have explained not only Valerie's words to me but why my mind was playing host to such strange thoughts and images. I dismissed what the teacher had said, and put it to the back of my mind.

Time passed quickly and it was soon 1983 and my time at Hethersett nearly up. After an assessment, I had been offered a place at the Royal National College for the Blind (RNC) in Hereford. The environment there was much like that of a university, with halls of residence and a student social club, and I was really excited at the prospect of going there. Some of my friends from Hethersett were going, too, and a couple of people I'd been at Jordanstown with were already there. This meant that I'd have a ready-made network of friends and wouldn't have to go through the wretched problems of that first term at Hethersett.

Before I left Hethersett however, two things happened in quick succession that were to bear out Valerie's words and turn my world upside.

I had gone to stay with a friend in Enfield, just north of London, for the weekend because I was attending a judo competition in the area. The family was listening to the news on television and I had one ear out but wasn't really paying much attention until an item was broadcast about a little girl who had gone missing. Her name was Marie Payne and it was thought that she had been abducted. As I listened to the reporter's voice I suddenly felt as if a scene from a film was being projected on to a screen in my mind. As I watched, the image of a silver car appeared, followed by outhouses and derelict buildings, a forest area and a lorry or van. The little girl's fear swept over me as if I were in her mind sharing her emotions, and the sensation of being in unfamiliar and hostile surroundings filled me with her dread.

Visualising a place that I had never seen physically, or been to, was a shock, but to be so tuned into the child was both terrifying and fascinating – I couldn't believe what was happening to me. I remembered my experiences at Jordanstown School where I could tune into my friends, but this was very different. I didn't know the little girl yet I had never received images with such clarity before – and what images! The vehicles and buildings were quite outside my experience.

I described what was happening to my friend and her parents, and her mother urged me to contact the police straight away as I was obviously getting a vision or message about what was happening to Marie. She thought I might be able to save the girl's life or help the police find her and bring her back to her family. The whole idea seemed crazy – the police weren't going to listen to a seventeen-year-old student – but in the end I was persuaded to make the call.

My friend's mother took me to the phone box and I dialed Scotland Yard.

'Um, I'm not sure if I can help, but I think I have some information for you...' I began.

My call was taken by a woman police officer and I told her what I had 'seen', fully expecting her to tell me off for wasting her time, but she didn't. She heard me through gravely and then thanked me for taking the time to call.

After the judo competition, I returned to Hethersett. I felt as if I'd done all I could for Marie, but didn't think I would hear any more about the incident. Two days later, I got a message to go to the headmaster's office. There, I found two detectives waiting to interview me; they wanted to talk to me about my phone call, and asked me to go down to the local police station with them because I had provided information that hadn't been released to the public.

Once at the police station, I was asked if I was prepared to go through my story again while hooked up to a lie detector. They explained that the machine worked by measuring the breathing, pulse and sweat emitted from the body, so I felt compelled to tell the operator that I studied yoga and could make my pulse and breathing slow down. The officer seemed pleased to have this information, but said that he thought the reading would be accurate, given that I could have kept the yoga a secret.

'Describe exactly what you saw and try to give us any more information if you can,' a detective said.

I told them what the girl looked like and that she was very scared. I could see the man holding her and gave a description of him and the concrete, windowless building she was being held in.

'Can you give us the man's name,' they pressed.

'I can only see initials,' I replied, 'a C and an E.'

Tragically, Marie's body was later found in Epping Forest in an area that matched my description. Colin Evans was convicted of her abduction and murder.

✳

This episode provided me with the first, overwhelming evidence that I could receive information beyond the physical senses. Up to now I had questioned everything that hadn't fitted in with what was rational, or what people around me considered rational. On one level it was a relief to find that my paranormal experiences were at last beginning to make sense to me; on another I felt uneasy at such a huge responsibility, especially at my age. What was I supposed to do with the information that was coming through?

Not long after this experience, I was to be given even more extensive proof that I had an extraordinary gift, and this time it related directly to my personal circumstances.

The assessment for entry into the RNC was a constant source of concern in those final months at Hethersett. It was impossible to prepare for. All I knew was that it would involve maths, English and interviews. Sat in my bedroom at Hethersett one day, studying and worrying over the assessment, a voice suddenly interrupted my thoughts, a voice that was instantly familiar.

'Sharon, I just want you to know that you *will* pass your assessment, so there's no need to worry.'

I froze. The husky voice that I hadn't heard since I was fourteen years old was my granny's.

'Granny, it can't be you!' I said aloud.

My immediate thought was that I was having some sort of a breakdown as a result of the stress of the impending assessment. If not that, then I'd fallen asleep and was dreaming. Yet this was no dream. I was wide awake, in my room.

Then I got another shock. I had recognised my grandmother immediately by her voice, but now for the first time in my life, I was looking at her. I could *see* her, standing in front of me with the kind smile that I had only ever before felt with my fingers. She was wearing a grey, black and white dress and a blue cardigan with the sleeves rolled up to her elbows.

A flood of emotions washed over me – happiness, surprise, sadness and curiosity.

'Let the family know I'm OK and I'm happy, and tell them not to grieve for me any more,' she said. I assured her I would pass this on, all the while guessing that the family would probably think I had gone mad. Maybe I had.

'Listen, Granny, am I imagining you're here because I'm under so much pressure?'

'No, Sharon,' she smiled again. 'I'm here, otherwise you wouldn't be able to see me.'

The logic of this cut through my confusion. I never knew what Granny looked like or what she wore so I wouldn't have been able to conjure her up in my mind.

'I've got to go now, but I'll always be looking after you,' Granny said, and then the image of her disappeared, leaving me in a state of complete confusion. On one level I was perplexed. I wasn't cracking up under the pressure of college; Granny had reassured me on that point. But how was Granny able to speak to me and project herself into my mind? Her voice had been as clear as day, the same as I remembered it, and she had been as real as if she had been standing next to me.

Because the experience was so intensely personal for me – being once again with the person I most loved in the world – I didn't immediately make the connection with my voices or any of the other unusual happenings. Furthermore, the impact of hearing Granny's voice initially obscured the greater significance of the event – that I had seen and talked to a spirit for the first time.

✳

I went home from Hethersett in July 1983 and eagerly waited for the results of my assessment. If Granny was right and I'd been accepted, I would start at the RNC in September that year. My aunts were keen, too, to know how I'd fared with the assessment.

'Oh, I've passed,' I said.

'You seem very confident,' laughed Aunt Roberta.

'Yes, I am. I saw Granny and she told me.'

This was the first time I had said anything to anyone about the apparition I'd seen in my room at college. I could imagine my aunt looking at me as if I were mad, but in a steady voice she reminded me that Granny was dead and could not possibly have spoken to me.

'So, what did she look like?' she added, probably thinking I wouldn't have an answer and that would be the end of it. Without hesitation I described Granny's features and what she had been wearing.

'That's my mummy down to a tee,' she gasped, astonished by the accurate description of someone I had never seen in life. Then the realisation that I had actually seen and spoken to a ghost sunk in. She was clearly frightened and hastily warned me, 'Sharon, don't you go too far with this – you don't know what you're getting into.'

Having my description confirmed was as much a surprise, and a shock, for me since it was also confirmation of what was becoming increasingly clear: that, just as the encyclopedia entry had stated, I was able to talk to the dead and receive information beyond the five senses. Everything that had happened was beginning to fall into place and become eerily real.

✳

There had also been another incident that is worth mentioning here. I couldn't explain it at the time, but in light of what had happened during those final months at Hethersett, I was now able to put it into context.

Throughout Boxing Day the previous Christmas I had been

picking up the smell of burning. My aunts did their best to reassure me – they hadn't left the cooker on or a cigarette burning in an ashtray. But the following day revealed a terrible tragedy.

During the night of Boxing Day, a fire had broken out at the house of a family friend, and her daughter, Martha, had died in the blaze. Only ten years old and suffering from asthma, the girl had been killed by smoke inhalation. This was an awful blow for the family and we were very distressed for them.

I went to the funeral and afterwards back to Martha's house. Her mother had another child, a son who was mentally disabled, and she suspected that Martha's brother had inadvertently set fire to the house when he was playing with the Christmas tree lights. I was able to tell her that this wasn't the case. I knew the fire had been ignited by a plug that had got water in it and started to smoulder. I told her about the smell I had received on Boxing Day, and I was also able to tell her that Martha was happy and resting. I don't know *how* I knew this – I'd never heard Martha's voice in the way that I had Granny's – but I was certain all the same.

The fire department later confirmed that the fire had indeed been caused by an electrical fault.

*

It seemed my yoga teacher was right when she predicted that events would unfold leading me to realise my psychic gifts. All the strange sensations, images and happenings that I had experienced during my young life were beginning to come together. The mystery was about to be solved, and I was finally to discover that I could use my gifts to help other people.

CHAPTER 7

Coming to Terms

—✳—

My three years at the Royal National College for the Blind were one of the happiest periods of my life. I was taking the Business and Technical Education Council Diploma (BTEC) course, which among other subjects covered consumer and business law, the structure of public and limited companies, and the subject I dreaded most, maths, along with others in my third year such as biology, which I loved. Ultimately, I was expecting to pursue some kind of career using my business studies qualifications or go into social work. We were given the chance to take extra-curricula courses outside college and encouraged to get involved in groups in the wider community, so I took advantage of this by taking a foundation course in counselling and becoming involved with the Samaritans, working on the phone lines. (I have since completed my training and become a qualified counsellor.)

People were always bringing their problems to me, even at Jordanstown, and my friends at the RNC looked upon me as the counsellor of the group. They would come and talk to me about anything that was worrying them, as would some of the teaching and domestic staff, despite there being a paid student counsellor at the college. It wasn't until I became more involved in my psychic work that I realised they were unconsciously tuning into my aura and could feel that I empathised with them.

One of the most important qualities a counsellor should possess is the ability to feel what the client is going through, to put themselves in that person's shoes but not to judge them. This came as second nature to me, but I could also recognise instinctively when people were holding things back from me and was able to fill in gaps and tell them what it was they were not divulging. I could put into words what the person was feeling and was able to explain certain aspects of their situation that they hadn't told me about.

On occasions, information from my unseen visitors would come into my head when I was talking to friends or counselling clients, but I had got used to this and didn't always listen to the visitors, although when I did they were invariably right. The fact is, I sometimes chose *not* to hear them. While I knew I had unusual skills, I was finding it hard to accept them as psychic gifts and to integrate them into my life. Despite all the evidence of my special powers, I couldn't work out the difference between the information provided by the voices and that generated by my own logic. This, I have since discovered, is one of the most common reasons why people who are developing their psychic abilities find the process confusing.

However, with practice, I began to make the distinction. When I was exercising my own powers of reasoning, I would receive information as thoughts in my head; when the information was coming from the voices, I would actually hear the words and they would be repeated over and over until I took them in. I still didn't know who my unseen visitors were, or why they had chosen me as a channel, but once again they took matters out of my hands.

As part of my studies, I had to write an essay on alternative religions and my views on how they were perceived by Western society, since most of them originated in the East. I had gone to the post office to collect my student grant only to find a queue stretching outside the door. I joined the end of it and was waiting patiently when my ears picked up a conversation two women were having about a small ad in the post office window for a local spiritualist meeting. They were laughing about it, joking about having to hold hands.

On an impulse, I interrupted them, told them I was in the middle of an essay on alternative religions and asked if they could write down the address of the meeting for me. The Circle of Light Spiritualist Church held its meetings every Sunday evening from 6.30 p.m. to 8 p.m.

This, I decided, would be a golden opportunity to get an interesting slant on my research and, armed with a tape recorder for taking notes, I got a taxi to what turned out to be a local hall, which is hired out to different groups. From a seat in the back row I waited to see what would happen.

After an opening hymn, prayers and a fifteen-minute talk given by the guest medium, the clairvoyant demonstration began. I never used the tape recorder – taking notes was to be the last thing on my mind.

The medium relayed various messages to the congregation that were supposed to have come from their dead relatives. I was a bit dubious about this, suspecting that she had been briefed with facts about members before the service or that people were planted in the congregation who would agree with whatever she said.

But then something extraordinary happened to me that bypassed my logic. I started to receive the messages before the medium delivered them from the platform. It was almost as if I was listening to a transcript of what the spirit people were telling her: I could identify the different accents and voices of the so-called spirits who were passing on their information. This was completely unexpected, and once again I wondered what was going on. Was I delusional, schizophrenic even? How was I able to intercept these voices? Yet, even as I asked myself these questions, it felt perfectly natural to be picking up on all this stuff.

Still, never one to accept anything at face value, I wanted to ask a lot more questions, and my opportunity came at the end of the service when the medium came over and introduced herself as Rosemary. I'd thought she was a guest at the hall that evening, but in fact she was a local medium and had noticed me because I was new. I explained about coming to take notes for my essay.

Her next words took me by surprise: 'How long have you had the gift?'

I pretended not to know what she was talking about, but understood perfectly what she meant – I'd been asked the same question by my yoga teacher at Hethersett. Rosemary, meanwhile, said that she was aware I'd been tuning into her on the platform and felt that I was a natural medium with an unusual power.

But I continued to insist that I didn't know what she was talking about. I'd heard about this sort of thing before, students being drawn into cults by persuasion and flattery, and then being brainwashed, and I wasn't having any of it.

'I'm not here to join some sort of cult,' I objected.

Rosemary patiently suggested I come to other meetings before reaching any conclusions, just to listen and perhaps learn more about what went on. Well, that didn't sound too sinister. She hadn't asked me to sign up to anything or hand over any money, and she hadn't stipulated any rules, so I decided I'd keep an open mind and take up her suggestion to go back again. After all, it was something different to do on a Sunday evening.

In the event, I didn't attend the meeting every week, but I went when I had time. Gradually I got to know other people who were in the process of developing their psychic powers. I also learned that, as children, they had had experiences similar to mine. They too had grown up hearing voices and seeing energy around people. And once again I felt a sense of relief. I wasn't mad after all.

At last I had come across people who could explain my unseen visitors to me: they were teachers and guides, men and women who had passed on and who were training me to communicate with the spirit world. My unseen visitors were guiding me to an understanding of how I might use my gifts to help people.

Yet I was still plagued by doubts. What was the point of the dead wasting their time trying to let everyone know they were watching over us? Why were some people chosen to be the messengers and not others? Was it just a case of a gullible congregation, too willing to believe that their loved ones were speaking to them? These were some of the questions I asked myself and put to others at this, the beginning of my journey of exploration into the psychic world.

Basically, I was taking an academic approach to the issues that were confronting me. Wearing my counsellor's hat, my feeling was that the mediums were preying on the vulnerable. People suffering from bereavement didn't need to hear about the dead living on when they leave this world. The bereaved needed to be encouraged to talk about their sense of loss and how this made them feel. How could holding out the false hope of meeting their loved ones some day possibly help them to come to terms with their grief?

These were some of the theories that ran through my mind as I wrestled with the dilemma of whether or not to accept my gift and to act on it.

One of the things that made me look at the problem from another point of view was the sincerity with which the mediums took the meetings. They were giving up their time voluntarily and for no recompense, and they came across as caring and compassionate. Something else that I couldn't dismiss was the 'survival evidence' (evidence that the spirit has survived) that was passed down from the platform – specific information from the spirit world, known only to the recipient, which is proof of communication with those who have passed on.

As far as the meeting being rigged was concerned, this did not hold up: messages would come through not only to regular members but to visitors as well. Nor could the comfort that these messages brought or the emotion they generated have been staged. In addition, the accuracy of some of the information was staggering. The mediums would relay personal details and information about how the deceased person had passed on that only the recipient could have known.

Then I started to look at the medium from the deceased relative's point of view. If I had passed on and there was some means of easing the pain of grief for friends and family left behind, would I want to be able to do that? Yes. I would certainly want to let them know that I was aware of what was happening in their lives and that I was watching over them. Clearly such reassurance would help to heal the wounds of grief and, more importantly, help people on earth understand that while our physical bodies may disintegrate when we die, we don't just fade away but live on in another state of consciousness. It would also be a comfort for them to know that they could meet up with their deceased relatives when they passed on, if they so desired.

I thought long and hard about all this, but the turning point came eventually when, one night, Rosemary invited me to give survival evidence in public. I had been sitting down among the congregation as usual when she asked me to come up to the platform. I thought she was joking, but she wasn't.

I had never done anything like this before. At college I'd started to discuss my dreams with close friends and they knew I was a little different; I'd even done a few readings – communicating with the spirit world – with them just for fun, to see if anything came through. But giving evidence in public to a spiritualist congregation was a completely different kettle of fish.

As I sat beside Rosemary, my legs were like jelly and my mouth was dry. I took a deep breath, cleared my mind and put my trust in my spirit guides. They didn't let me down. For five or ten minutes I was able to relay messages to people in the audience, and whatever I said – it all passed in such a haze – they understood. It was a most humbling experience. A feeling of love and support, both from my unseen visitors and from the congregation in the church, overwhelmed me. But more than that, I was conscious of the huge sense of relief of those in the spirit world whose messages I'd been able to carry.

In that moment I realised the healing power of my gift, and I knew that I wanted more than anything to use it to play my part in giving help and comfort to those who needed it. Those five or ten minutes were life changing.

I can imagine how frustrating my resistance must have been for those on the spirit side who had nurtured me from childhood. How they must have celebrated!

*

Once I had accepted my gift, I began to use it. Even though I was in the early stages of my psychic development, I made use of my powers more frequently alongside my counselling training to help my clients, though I was careful not to mention this to them.

I suspect that many good counsellors are psychic, but we are not supposed to mix counselling and psychic skills. However, I strongly believe that both skills should work in conjunction and in many cases do. Many professional mediums have counselling qualifications, and this training can be extremely useful. Mediums who are not able to recognise underlying psychological problems have been known to cause nervous breakdowns in vulnerable people.

And not everyone who hears voices is a potential medium; it can also be a symptom of a personality disorder such as schizophrenia. It is vitally important to know the difference between psychic ability and psychological disturbance.

I also know of people who have joined development circles (psychic schools) in order to train to use their psychic abilities and then ended up in a psychiatric ward because they couldn't cope with what they were experiencing. Again, it is essential that mediums who run these circles question participants closely about their childhood experiences, family history and so on, in case there is a history of psychological problems in the family. Why, for example, does the person want to become a medium in the first place? What sort of experiences are they having? They should be asked to describe in detail the type of communication they are receiving and the pattern it takes. Does it happen at specific times or randomly? What sort of message does the spirit pass to the participant and how is the message manifest?

A lot of useful information can be gleaned from the answers

to these questions. I remember a consultation with a man who had tried to open himself up to his psychic abilities by reading a manual on psychic development. He explained that the spirits who were communicating with him were aggressive and would tell him that his friends and family thought he was a failure and didn't love or respect him. This plunged him into a depression and he had resorted to drugs and self-harm to eradicate the frustration and anger that these revelations triggered.

I urged him to seek professional help from his doctor because I knew he was not receiving spirit communication at all but suffering from mental problems, released by his do-it-yourself attempt to open his mind.

In this case, it was obvious that my client wasn't in touch with spirits. It is highly unlikely that anyone who is genuinely in communication with the spirit world would receive such destructive messages. However, not every case is as clear cut and, when dealing with potential students, mediums need to be guided by their instincts as well as by the advice they are given by their own guides from the spirit world.

Yet, conversely, I do believe that some patients who are treated for psychological conditions may be receiving communication from the spirit world. And it would be no bad thing for psychologists and psychiatrists to study the theory of mediumship when they are assessing patients in order to rule out this possibility. These professionals need to be more open to the fact that a patient can in fact be receiving messages from spirits. Mediums should be used to work alongside health professionals when patients in psychiatric units are being assessed as only mediums have the skills to tune into patients on a psychic level.

Alas, one of the basic problems with psychology and psychiatry is that psychic abilities are not accepted by the medical professions. Psychologists will maintain that belief in a world beyond ours is wishful thinking. They will argue that when we dream about meeting and talking to loved ones it is the subconscious trying to work through, and end, the grieving process.

I disagree with this theory and can speak from personal experience. As a neutral channel of communication and for the benefit of their loved ones left behind, I can talk to many people who have passed on, but I still can't talk to my own grandparents. It is too emotional for me. So they usually come to me when I am in the dream state and pass any messages to me then. It is common to dream of meeting loved ones who have passed on and for them to communicate with us in dreams. This is because it is easier for them to come to us when we are relaxed and therefore more receptive and less likely to be frightened.

This was precisely why my unseen voices approached me first in my dreams when I was a child, though I sometimes wonder why they didn't back off immediately when I got frightened. Perhaps they simply miscalculated. But, with hindsight, I think it was a strategic move on their part. If the voices hadn't come to me when I was so young and impressionable I might not later have connected the nightmares with other unusual happenings in my life and would not have realised the voices were part of a bigger plan. I was only frightened because I didn't know who they were. They, however, knew this was just the beginning for me; there was far more powerful evidence of the spirit world to be revealed.

✳

As my own psychic development continued, I learned that I could use my abilities to help people, not just in the meetings, but with private readings. These are one-to-one sessions conducted in private, rather like a consultation, and I continued to practise on my friends – more for fun than anything else – clearing my mind and waiting for someone to come through to me from the spirit world with a message for the person with me. It was tricky at first because I had to learn to distinguish between my own thoughts and the information I was getting from my voices. I quickly learned to rely on the voices, however, as the information I received from them was pretty accurate.

There is a particular case that sticks in my mind. A student came to me for a reading but was very dubious about my talents. He wasn't one of my friends so I didn't know anything about him, and not knowing what he looked like either I had no non-verbal clues. His name was English so I assumed that he was English, but I was wrong. As I listened to my voices, I discovered that he had lived in Singapore as a child and I was able to give him information about the precise area as well as details about his grandmother who had passed on. He had come to my room very sceptical; he left completely baffled. Soon word about my readings spread around the college and, much to my amusement, I gradually earned myself the nickname of 'The Fortune Teller'.

✳

One night Jenny, the warden of my hall of residence, knocked on my bedroom door during her routine rounds. As she was about to leave my room, I suddenly heard a voice in my head: 'Mary wants to thank Jenny for everything she is doing and wish her well.'

I hesitated. How would Jenny react to receiving such a message from me? Would she even know who Mary was? I hardly knew Jenny at that stage because I had only recently arrived at the college, but I made up my mind to run with my instincts.

'I know you're going to think this is crazy,' I said to her, 'but I have a message for you from Mary. She wants to thank you for everything you are doing and she wishes you well.' I was expecting Jenny to laugh and tell me she hadn't a clue who I was talking about. Instead she gasped, 'How did you know about Mary?'

Explaining that Mary had just spoken to me, I asked Jenny who she was. Jenny said she was doing research for a book she was writing about a woman called Mary Morgan, who had been the last woman to be hanged in Wales for infanticide.

This amazed and intrigued me at the same time. I wanted to learn more about it and also I felt compelled to act as the mouthpiece for Mary in Jenny's research – I knew that this was why Mary had given me the message to pass on.

It was still early days in my psychic journey, but the conviction that Mary really wanted me to tell the story from her point of view was thrilling. Over the next few months I was able to provide new information about exactly what had happened and why Mary had been forced to kill her baby.

Mary Morgan had been employed as the servant at Maesllwch Castle in Wales, the seat of the local Member of Parliament, but the gentleman's son had raped her then threatened her with dismissal if she told anyone about what had happened. So Mary kept silent, but she also found she was pregnant. Terrified and alone, she delivered the baby herself in her attic room, and knowing that she couldn't keep the child, took a hunting knife that belonged to the child's father, barricaded herself in the attic with a mattress against the door and slit the baby's throat. The knife handle was engraved with the letter W for Walter, the name of Mary's abuser.

When they found Mary in her room and realised what she had done she was tried and sentenced to hang for her crime. Many local people were aware of the injustice taking place, and the hangman refused to do the job, so a man with a horse and cart was persuaded to attach Mary's legs to the horse and drag on the rope while Mary was suspended from a tree.

As I spoke to Mary and relayed her story to Jenny, I ran the gamut of emotions Mary would have felt, right down to the horrifying sensation of being hanged. It was a petrifying experience, yet afterwards, I felt an overwhelming sense of release and peace from Mary. I felt that she had finally been put to rest.

Jenny subsequently took me with her on a visit to the town where all this happened, but I had no desire to stay for long as I could feel Mary's emotional energy all over the place.

CHAPTER 8

Meeting the Team

—*—

Like a young bird trying out its wings, I continued to flex my psychic skills, practising readings on the students and staff at the RNC and, during the holidays, on friends and family back in Belfast. Occasionally I'd try my hand at predicting, with rather mixed results. We were due to move in 1984, and I foresaw that the number of the new house would be between 30 and 36, it was 34. I said we would move between January and April and we moved in February.

I certainly didn't hit anywhere near the mark every time. I predicted, for example, that Frank Bruno would win a boxing match and my family put money on it. He lost. Luckily I hadn't made a bet, and the family saw the funny side of it. I don't make predictions for monetary gain because I feel it's wrong, but that was just a bit of fun. I should say here that, much as I would like to, the ability to predict their own future is not something that is given to psychics. The gift I have been given is intended to benefit others.

In more recent years, predictions have sometimes featured in readings with clients, but this depends always on what comes through from the spirit world, it is nothing to do with tarot or the stars. On one occasion, I was able to tell a client, Joanne, that she would marry and have three children but that her second child would be overdue and that the labour would be difficult. I also told her that she would change her career – she was a personal assistant at the time – and move into education, though not as a teacher. Joanne was adamant that she was perfectly happy where she was. A few years later she came for another reading and told me that my predictions about her life had been accurate in every respect and that she was now working as a school secretary after her previous job had terminated.

✳

The family began to believe in my gift when I told them about the vision I'd had of Granny, but I hadn't taken them into my confidence over my abilities or the fact that I was exploring them, and we never talked much about my time at college. They were always right behind me, however. They encouraged me to keep doing what I thought was right for me and fully supported me when I started doing readings at home. I think they were genuinely delighted that I had found my niche, even if it was only a hobby at that stage. The idea of my becoming a medium certainly didn't seem to frighten them. My mum believed in what I was doing too, at least she did until she became a 'born again' Christian; from then on she refused to discuss it.

Back at the RNC, I was about to mark another milestone in my psychic journey. I met two women who ran a meditation group once a week from their home. For me it was the perfect opportunity to try an aspect of the yoga classes that I had so enjoyed, but it turned out to be another case of fortunate synchronicity.

It was while I was sitting meditating that I felt moved to find out who my unseen visitors were. The time had come for a critical step forward in my development.

Acceptance of my voices as a reality had gradually become easier for me. With all the evidence at the spiritualist meetings and my readings at college, I could no longer ignore them or dismiss them as a figment of my imagination and was increasingly turning to them in my psychic work. It was high time I found out more.

The members of the meditation group included healers and one or two people who had experience with psychic development, so I knew the group would be a safe environment for this next step. I'm quite convinced that my teacher and guides, who I now call 'my team', were steering me towards initiating a conversation with them. Up until that time they had given me messages and images, but I hadn't communicated with them. Once we started talking, our communication flowed smoothly in both directions, as if it were the most natural thing in the world.

The first person to introduce himself was Doctor Jim Foster. He had been born in Clydebank in Glasgow and had trained as a general practitioner at Glasgow University, later moving to Bristol where he died while on his way to see a patient in a car accident in 1945 just before the Second World War ended. I realised that he had been the source of the information about biology that I'd been given at school and about the condition of casualties when I was in the Red Cross.

There had even been an occasion when Jim's instructions had helped me save a life. While I was still at school in Belfast, I was awakened one night by one of my aunts who was in the bathroom screaming with the pain of a violent headache. It was so bad that she was banging her head against the wall. I heard a voice telling me to apply alternate hot and cold cloths to her head. When the doctor came he said that my quick action had probably saved her life; a blood clot had lodged in her brain but the application of the hot and cold cloths had shifted it. (I didn't tell my aunt that I had been given the information psychically, just that I had learned it on my first-aid course.)

My spirit teacher is Little Eagle, a Zulu warrior chief, who I call 'the Chief'. His has a key role in my life since he is responsible for answering any questions I have about my spiritual development. This questioning and probing of a medium's guides and spirit team is a crucial part of psychic growth – how else are we to learn? He also helps me with this aspect of my own teaching in development groups. The Chief has told me that he has been with me from my birth and will be there to meet me when I pass on.

Individual members of my spirit team have come and gone over the years, according to the stage I am at in my psychic development, much as one has different teachers in different years at school. It depends too on the individual spirit, their choices and their needs. But both Jim and the Chief are constant companions and work with me to this day. When I've had private sittings with other mediums, and even at public demonstrations of mediumship when other psychics are present, they have often mentioned seeing Jim and the Chief near me. I have so much to thank them both for, particularly their patience and perseverance during the years when I wouldn't acknowledge them or accept my gifts. Yet, lengthy and confusing as my apprenticeship was, I now feel it was meant to be, it had a purpose: I had to go through it in order that I could explain to others developing their abilities about the process of getting to know the spirit teams who work with them.

You don't have to be a psychic or medium to have a spirit team – everyone has a spirit guide and team whether they realise it or not. I have got to know my team well and am familiar with the functions they perform. There are nine spirits who work closely with me, though I can draw on extra help if and when I need to.

And from time to time I have needed to. One occasion was in 1995 when I was on holiday with my family in Majorca. We had gone for a drive into the mountains, but on the way back a thick mist descended and we got hopelessly lost. The map indicated two possible routes, but it was an old map and the roads weren't clearly marked. What were we going to do? We couldn't get a signal for our mobile phones as we were in the middle of two mountain ranges and it was getting late. Suddenly, I heard a voice telling me to put my hands over the map. It wasn't one of my regular team, but I followed his instructions anyway as he seemed to know the area well and was able to show me the best way back. I learned later that my guide had been a member of a mountain rescue patrol in Majorca who had passed on. As he indicated the route to me, I pointed it out on the map to my aunt. Following his directions we soon got out of the mountains safely and I thanked him for his help. My team told me they had asked him to help us out.

This guide was Spanish, and I should point out here that language is not a barrier when we are communicating with the spirit world. Communication can be transmitted by thought, images and sensations as well as by voice, depending on the communicator from the spirit world and on the circumstances.

Each team member has a unique role to play. Two of them were doctors while on earth and they still advise in this capacity now: in addition to Jim, there is Simon who had been a distinguished cardiologist. I met Simon in spirit through a client who came to me for a reading. She had known him when he was alive, and after he died he gave her survival evidence during the reading with me.

A few weeks after the reading with my client, Simon contacted me because he felt he could help me to carry out my work more effectively, especially the healing aspect. Along with Jim, he is also responsible for monitoring my own energy levels when I am on stage or doing private readings.

Gerard was a community psychiatric nurse who lived in Cork. He has been invaluable in my work with clients who may need counselling or help on a psychological level, although Gerard's involvement is never something I would discuss with a client.

He has also provided invaluable support on a personal level as someone I can discuss my feelings with. This is essential for anyone involved in psychic work, much as it is in psychology and psychiatry. Psychics and mediums tend to put their own emotions on the back burner so they can better address their clients' problems and emotions by being completely professional and objective. But psychics are not made of stone; we are physical beings like everyone else, and repressing our feelings can lay up considerable problems for us in the future.

It would be really useful if there was a helpline for mediums and psychics so that they could share and discuss things with others involved in similar work, and perhaps be given support and advice about psychic development. A helpline is one of several projects that I am hoping to follow up at some stage.

Other projects include a psychic foundation that takes a non-visual approach to developing psychic skills in order to encourage blind people to get involved, and my own investigational television programme devoted to my area of work.

✻

Among my team there are also my spirit 'bouncers'. All three lived in Belfast but I never knew them when they were on earth. My right-hand man is Patrick Campbell. He lost his life in tragic circumstances in Dublin, and I continue to be in close contact with his family as his uncle is my friend and manager.

The job of my bouncers is to keep things calm and orderly on the spirit side when I am communicating during readings or on stage. They have to ensure that only one person from the spirit world speaks to me at a time. Sometimes the communicators can be so eager to pass on messages to friends and family on earth that they will all try to come through at the same time, which can be extremely confusing, if not alarming, for the medium. My bouncers handle this by forming the communicators into a queue, just as they might in the physical world, and introducing them to me one at a time. Other mediums who have been in the audience at my shows have often seen this happen.

Things can occasionally get a bit rowdy, and there are times when the bouncers have to break up arguments between communicators on the other side. Once, I was giving a reading to a man who had lost his girlfriend in a car accident. He had been in the car too and had told the police that the girl had been driving at the time of the accident. This wasn't true. Towards the end of the reading the girl came through, not at all pleased about the false accusation against her. I explained to the man that she knew he'd lied about who was driving the car that night. He was astounded.

But the young woman carried on communicating through me, calling her erstwhile boyfriend some choice names, which I couldn't repeat, and that was when the argument started on the other side. Suddenly, the man's grandparents turned up on the spirit side wanting their tuppence worth and remonstrating with the girl over the insults to their grandson.

I couldn't explain this to my client, so I waited until order had been restored on the other side. Patrick and the others separated the grandparents and the girlfriend and told them they would have to leave.

It was in fact one of my bodyguards who originally suggested I should have a team to manage security from a spiritual angle. When he was on earth, Steve (not his real name) used to scoff at the idea of psychics, mediums and the spirit world. He lived in Belfast and, just like me, came from a working-class background, but he grew up in West Belfast, in the area of the city most affected by the Troubles. His opinion of the psychic world changed when he watched a documentary I made in 1995. The programme made a deep impression on Steve. He knew that in his line of business he was running serious risks, and he told his family to contact me should anything happen to him, promising that he would make an effort to contact them. Shortly after this, he lost his life. He had failed to heed a warning about drug dealing and had been shot in a power struggle. He was still only in his twenties.

Steve's family came to see me privately and I was able to pass on details about his life and death that confirmed his identity. After the reading they told me what Steve had said about getting in touch with me. The idea that the documentary could have made such an impact on someone so young moved and surprised me.

Later, Steve himself contacted me to say that he would be interested in working as a member of my spirit team. His proposal was to provide security for me, to make sure that I was protected both physically and spiritually. As well as keeping the communicators in order, Steve thought I might need protection when I was carrying out rescue work – clearing haunted properties – which I do need from time to time.

✳

Most people who pass on have no problem in making the transition from earth to the spirit world, but there are those who find it difficult at first. They don't realise they are dead and continue to hang around, or haunt, the places they were familiar with while on earth. They will try to attract the attention of the living by causing what is known as 'activity' – moving objects and furniture, opening drawers and doors and turning on water taps – and cannot understand why they are being ignored. If the spirit is restless there is usually a feeling of intense cold in the property, even though the heating may be on.

The intention is rarely to frighten those on earth but merely to let them know they are around. However, there are exceptions to the rule. A few years ago, I was called in to deal with a haunted property in Belfast where the spirit of a man had been seen and heard. It seemed that he had taken a fancy to the woman who lived there with her husband and two children, and though he didn't bother the woman herself or the children, he had a problem with her husband. The spirit kept pulling the duvet from the side of the bed where the man slept, and opening his wardrobe door and disturbing his clothes. The family would also hear laughter and abusive language coming from the walls. Happily, I was able to talk to the spirit and make him understand that he had to leave.

A spirit might occasionally become more aggressive. I clearly recall being thrust against a bedroom door by one man who didn't want to leave a house, but my team swiftly leapt into action, standing between us and surrounding him.

My job is to try to communicate with the spirit beings that inhabit a building and explain to them that they have passed on from the physical world, which is why they aren't attracting the attention of the living beings. Sometimes it's as simple as that and they will leave the premises because they don't want to be there any more either. In these cases my spirit team will help them cross to the spirit world where they will be reunited with their own departed loved ones. It is very rare that force is needed to move them on.

*

When Steve first approached me he explained that he wanted to do this kind of work as his way of making up for the life he had led on earth. Young though he was, he had been a hard man, handy with his fists, feared by many and completely without fear himself, thinking nothing of single-handedly taking on several men at a time.

Steve's experience shows that when we pass on, we are given the chance to redeem ourselves. No matter what we have done on earth, no matter how horrible the crime, there is always the opportunity to change our ways, to atone for what wrongs we have done and to turn things around from negative to positive. The important thing is that we take responsibility for our actions, admit when we have done something wrong and try to make amends.

The common word for this balancing of the scales of one's actions is 'karma'. Every major religion teaches the same principle, but there are different interpretations of how karma works. Eastern religions teach us that we live by cause and effect – what we reap we sow – and I think they have got it about right. The Christian religion teaches that we can be forgiven if we pray for forgiveness; to my mind this is far too easy. How can we expect the slate to be wiped clean just because we pray for someone to do it for us? I would prefer to take responsibility for what I have done and try to make up for it. But everyone is entitled to their own opinion on these matters, and they will believe whatever is right for them.

I'm so pleased to have been instrumental in helping Steve come to realise that violence is not a satisfactory way of achieving one's goals, and though he can still be tough when necessary, he now deals with tricky situations very sensitively.

My third 'bouncer' died in similar circumstances to Steve; indeed, it was Steve who introduced us. They both love the work they are doing and their families on the earth are aware that they are part of my team. They are free to move on from my team at any time but it appears they don't wish to, and I feel sure we will be working together for a long time to come.

While most of my team have only passed on within the last twenty years, three of them have been in the spirit world for some 2,000 years or more. The Chief is one of these, then there is Harem Toot Rah, who was an Egyptian oracle, and the third, also an Egyptian, is a woman called Guiveraugh. The Chief introduced me to Guiveraugh, and I was able to verify her existence independently. She told me about two books in which she is mentioned, and I have since come by copies of these. She was a warrior queen in Egypt and came to Britain thousands of years ago where she was killed in battle. Guiveraugh helps me with difficult rescue work and sends me energy when I need a boost.

Harem Toot Rah was introduced to me by a psychic artist while I was at a psychic fair in Cork in 2002. Toot is mainly involved in helping me communicate messages correctly; he is not around me quite as much as the other members of my team.

Working with the team is exactly the same as working in a group situation in the physical world. Each individual has their own personality, just as they had on earth. Guiveraugh, for example, is a strong, no-nonsense kind of person who doesn't suffer fools gladly and gets on with the job. Jim is a man of few words, but whatever he says speaks volumes. Gerard is a deep thinker who analyses every situation carefully.

Patrick is and was a real joker. One Halloween his family was gathered together at his mother's house when a figure swathed in white bandages appeared at the window. Screaming in fright, they scurried to the other end of the room but the figure followed them to another window. It turned out to be Patrick, wrapped in bandages, disguised as an Egyptian mummy. On another occasion he dressed a doll in christening robes and pretended to drop it on the floor, to the horror of his family who thought it was his baby cousin who had been christened that day.

Patrick, too, lost his life in violent circumstances though he was never involved with drugs. In fact, he hated them and anyone who dealt in them, so it's quite ironic that he should now be working alongside people who were involved in them in life. It proved quite difficult for him at first, but the team is very close now even if they do have the occasional argument. It's also somewhat ironic that he should be working with me since, as his family has told me, it's unlikely we would ever have kept company in life because he would have been too frightened of my psychic gifts.

He still messes around in spirit as he did in life, although he has his serious side. When I am feeling down, Patrick always knows what to say to make me laugh, and his family is very proud of the valuable work he is doing now.

I greatly appreciate the help of my team and thank them for it every day. They are not just my guides, but my friends too. They have seen me through both good times and bad, helping me negotiate many of life's little inconveniences as well as some of its major downturns.

People sometimes ask why, if the spirits communicate with me over fairly inconsequential matters, they haven't stopped me from making stupid decisions, or warned me about misplaced trust, or, for example, why they didn't diagnose my Granny's illness so that she didn't have to die so young.

It's a question that is difficult to answer, but I believe that we have a predestined pathway in life and that certain things should not be altered as they might deflect our spiritual evolution. To evolve we need to learn, and if we got help from the spirits with everything, we would never progress on our life's path. The spirits are not there to interfere with life's lessons. Some things have to happen. If my grandmother had not died when she did, I would not have gone to Hethersett in England, and I might never have become a medium. Similarly, Granny's own spiritual evolution might have been interrupted.

In fact, my team does send me warnings on rare occasions, and I do well to take note. In the late 1980s, I had an evening booking at an address in Belfast for a group reading. Throughout the day I got messages from my team urging me not to go. I didn't ignore them but I felt bound to honour my booking. Normally I'd receive a confirmation call, but in this instance no one rang me and in the end I tried to phone the person who'd made the booking. The number did not exist. So I asked a taxi driver friend of mine to check out the address. It turned out to be a derelict building. To this day I don't know if the booking was a hoax or something more sinister.

CHAPTER 9

On the Receiving End

——✳——

Whilst I was at the RNC, the two women who ran the meditation group rented a room at weekends at the local health centre to offer healing to the public, and I thought it might be a good idea to join them in their healing practice. This was so that I could develop my healing skills further. I had never been trained as a healer but knew I had a gift for it; it was easy for me to tell when a client was in pain and I seemed to know instinctively where to place my hands to give relief.

Healing takes a variety of forms. The technique I use is based on channelling energy and often called 'spiritual healing', though I prefer just 'healing'. The energy originates not in me but in the cosmos, the universal energy source, and is transmitted through me to the client by my spirit doctors, Jim, Simon and another physician, Chris, who I draw on for extra help. I will usually stand behind my client and check out their aura so that my spirit helpers can make a diagnosis – I'm not a doctor. Then, placing my hands on their shoulders, I will work down the arms, chest and upper back, spine and finally the head, with sweeping downward movements. The healing works by triggering the body's responses into action.

It was at these weekend healing sessions that I first met Margaret, a woman in her thirties who had suffered a stress-induced stroke that affected the muscles on her right side, though she was able to walk and hold a conversation. I started a course of counselling and healing with her and we became close friends, meeting up when I had spare time to go into town for coffee or get together at college.

Although she still easily became depressed, after a few months she seemed to be making good progress and had improved considerably. I was then living in lodgings with one of the staff who worked at the college – students in their third year lived in lodgings so they could get a taste of living independently. My landlady had given me permission to use her telephone number for emergencies because of my healing and counselling work, as long as the calls did not come in after a certain time at night. However, she disapproved fundamentally of my work, covering this up by admonishing me for not having more friends my own age (in fact I did have plenty of friends at college).

One Saturday afternoon I was in my room studying. Margaret and I had arranged to meet up at my digs the next day and I wanted to clear the decks of some college work beforehand. I was looking forward to seeing her. While I was occupied, Margaret telephoned and asked to speak to me, but my landlady told her I was out. When Margaret didn't turn up on the Sunday, I didn't think to worry, I just imagined she had wanted to spend the day with her family instead, and anyway I knew she'd be in touch the following weekend.

Next day I was relieving the college switchboard operator so she could take a lunch break – this wasn't compulsory but I enjoyed manning the switchboard and would help her out if I could – when a woman called and asked for a message to be delivered to Sharon Neill. I couldn't tell her that she was speaking to me because we weren't allowed to reveal our identity to callers on the switchboard, but said I would make sure she got the message.

The message knocked me sideways. 'Please tell Sharon that Margaret was found yesterday in her home. She had taken an overdose. She didn't survive. There was a letter to the family and she asked us to let Sharon know she had phoned on Saturday but Sharon wasn't available.' The caller was Margaret's sister.

I got through the rest of the shift on autopilot, then went and sat on a bench outside the lecture halls where a member of staff eventually found me and took me to the sick bay. The nurse made me lie down and gave me a cup of tea. I was totally devastated.

Why had Margaret's message not been delivered to me at my lodgings? Perhaps I could have said or done something that might have stopped my friend from taking her life.

After the funeral, I phoned Margaret's sister – I had met her once and she'd been really pleased with how I was helping Margaret. She assured me that neither she nor the family felt I was in any way to blame. Margaret had stocked up on anti-depressants with the intention of using them to end her life.

Nevertheless, I continued to feel very distressed by the situation. I had no reason to suspect Margaret would do anything like this, but I still felt guilty about not calling her back that Sunday morning. I had helped many people who were suicidal, but this was different: the others had been strangers, Margaret was my friend and I had failed her.

With these thoughts revolving in my mind, I came to the conclusion that I had to give up my psychic and counselling work. If it hadn't been for them I wouldn't have met Margaret and she might still be alive. I felt I should have known, either professionally or empathetically, and anticipated what Margaret was going to do. If I couldn't help people put their lives back together, there wasn't any point in carrying on. What I failed to take into account, though, was how young and comparatively inexperienced I was at that stage.

A short while afterwards I went to one of my Sunday spiritualist meetings with the intention of telling the healing and meditation groups about my decision. As it happened, the service was being taken by a guest medium. Almost immediately, she pointed to me, unaware that I was blind, and said she had a message for me.

'I have a woman who had recently passed on through suicide. Her name is Margaret. Do you understand?'

I was astonished and overcome with emotion. The medium couldn't have known this, nor could she have been forewarned by any other member of the congregation since they didn't know what had happened.

Tears streamed down my face as the medium continued with her message.

'Margaret is at peace now. She doesn't want you to give up your work because of her. She says she would have taken the tablets anyway. You will carry on your work and will help many thousands of people in the future, and Margaret will always be watching over you from the spirit world.'

This was a turning point for me in my grief at Margaret's death, and at the end of the service, I told the medium how grateful I was for the message and explained the circumstances.

She in turn comforted me greatly; there would be many people I wouldn't be able to help in my work, she said, but the number would be small compared to the help and comfort I could bring to many others.

But that day it was my turn to be at the receiving end of the powerful comfort that mediumship can bring, and as I left the meeting I felt that a great weight had been lifted from me. The message from Margaret and my conversation with the medium had driven away all thoughts of giving up my work.

The other lesson I learned from that experience is that you can only do so much to help someone; if they still choose to harm themselves it is their decision, and one must not feel responsible for their actions.

The message from Margaret made me truly appreciate the solace mediums all over the world give to countless numbers of people by providing them with survival evidence from loved ones on the other side. Receiving unmistakable proof that someone you have known on earth has passed on from the physical world and is still alive in spirit is the most wonderful feeling imaginable, because it is evidence that your loved ones are able to see what's going on in your life and share memories that only they can know. Indeed, I know Margaret is watching over me because she has since contacted me directly.

Later that year, at college, something happened that reinforced Margaret's message to me about carrying on with my work: I was to be instrumental in saving a friend's life.

Students were offered work experience in the college office to give them a flavour of a real office environment, and one morning, while I was working a shift there and about to have a cup of tea with a colleague, I suddenly had an overwhelming urge to go and see Sarah, a student friend of mine, in her room. She was younger than me and still lodged in the halls of residence. Asking my colleague to cover for me, I hurried to Sarah's room and knocked on the door. There was no answer, but the door was on the latch so I went in. Sarah was lying on the bed semiconscious with an empty tablet bottle on the floor beside her.

'How did you know? I don't want to live any more,' she mumbled as I knelt down to take her pulse. 'How did you know what I did?'

I knew she needed help, so told her to keep calm while I went to phone the nurse. Sarah was taken to hospital and, much to my relief, she survived.

If there had been any doubt in my mind, I knew now that I couldn't give up my work because of one bad experience.

CHAPTER 10

Medical Interventions

——✳——

I left the RNC in July 1986 and returned home to Belfast to live with my grandfather and aunts, determined to continue my psychic work. A splinter group had broken away from the main spiritualist church in Northern Ireland, and was being run by a fantastic medium and healer, Isabel Ewing. I decided this was the right place for me. As in Hereford, the services were held in a hired hall every Sunday evening, and Isabel also held a healing group at her house. I joined both and started taking services and giving healing.

I also started my first proper job, in August 1986, as a telephonist for the Housing Executive in Belfast (the same as a housing association in England), but it wasn't long before a mystery illness put me out of action, both physically and spiritually. The trouble started with a throat infection, and eventually I lost my voice completely, which made it impossible to work on the telephones.

The infection would clear up for four or five days and then come back again; meanwhile, I started to get dizzy spells. I would be walking across the floor and fall over for no reason. My family couldn't leave me in the house alone unless I was lying down. Once, when they had to leave me for half an hour or so to go to the shops, they came back to find me lying on the living room floor – I'd tried to answer the phone, been overcome by a dizzy spell, fallen and hit my head on the coffee table.

The trouble persisted so my doctor referred me to a consultant. He couldn't find anything wrong with me. Instead he tried to persuade me that my illness was all in my imagination and that I was simply falling over because I was blind. I may have been blind but I wasn't stupid, and none of this squared up with my previous history. I had never fallen over before and was in fact very steady on my feet. The doctors proceeded to test me for everything from anaemia to leukaemia but drew a complete blank – the results always came back normal.

It seemed I would have to let the illness run its course, and it finally cleared up in March the following year, but by then I'd had to give up the Housing Executive job. Throughout this time I had heard nothing from my spirit team, who, as I found out later, couldn't contact me because all my energies were being used to fight the mystery condition.

In the event, the illness cleared up as suddenly as it had started. The most likely cause was stress. I had been doing so much at college, mentally, physically and spiritually, that it seemed I had finally burned out.

That summer, I was offered another position at the Housing Executive. This time my problems started before I had even had a chance to put a foot across the threshold. Two days before I was due to take up the job, I went to the dentist for an emergency appointment as I was having trouble with my gums. I thought it was an abscess but in fact it was my wisdom teeth, and the dentist sent me straight to an orthodontist. The wisdom teeth, all four of them, had to come out under anaesthetic; the teeth were beginning to come through but my mouth was too small to accommodate them, and this was what was causing the pain.

All I remembered was going into the dentist's — I don't remember coming out. Apparently my aunts had to carry me downstairs and put me into the car. Unfortunately, my mouth haemorrhaged while I was sleeping, and because both sides of my gums were stitched up, I developed an infection and had to go on antibiotics. But I managed to turn up for the first day of my new job, and while I must have looked an awful mess with my bruised and swollen face, my boss took it in his stride.

This time I was working in the maintenance depot as a clerical officer. I was the only woman among about 150 men, and I loved it. They treated me like a queen, bringing me fizzy drinks and chocolate bars — if I'd eaten everything they gave me I would have weighed a ton.

Again I found myself in the position of counsellor, since many of the men would come and confide their problems in me, particularly relationship and domestic troubles. Because of my previous experience, they put me in charge of the First Aid room and I also dealt with any minor accidents that cropped up in the depot.

(Sadly, I lost the job in 1990 for making personal phone calls during working hours. I was one of the unlucky ones who got caught, but it was my own fault and a lesson usefully learned.)

My days at the depot were busy and happy ones, and in the evenings I carried out private readings from home where I had bought a caravan to use as a consulting room — no scarves and dangly earrings for me though. To start with, I'd placed an advertisement in the local paper, and this was all that was needed: my client base grew steadily from word of mouth, both for the readings and the healing clinic that I held once a week.

I never charged for any of my work while I was at college, and even at this stage I only took donations for the healing and a nominal fee for the readings, since I had a full-time job and my psychic activities were still really just a hobby.

The clients who came to me for healing ranged in age from nine to eighty. There was a little girl who was having hearing problems because of fluid behind the eardrum. She'd been attending hospital for treatment but the medication wasn't working. A few weeks after I started treatment, the fluid started to dissolve and the treatment was successful.

A man came to me with an inoperable tumour on his lung. I didn't expect to be able to do anything for him except ease the pain, but I was in for a surprise. When he went back to hospital for an X-ray, they found the tumour had shrunk and he was able to have it removed. This was wonderful news and I was delighted I had been able to help him, though I could never take all the credit for the healing or the readings. I could do nothing without my spirit team.

Word of my work spread further and I started going out to clients' houses as well as conducting readings from home. My first visit was in West Belfast, and reminded me what a strange and fractured world Northern Ireland was. While I was sitting in the bedroom of the flat giving a reading, a helicopter flew low overhead. My immediate thought was that there was going to be trouble. My client laughed and told me it was a regular occurrence in that area, where the army used helicopters to sweep for, and monitor, any unusual activity. In East Belfast we rarely saw helicopters and were hardly affected by the Troubles.

✳

For a reading, which is sometimes called a 'sitting' by the spiritualist churches, I like to have the client on my right side because it makes it easier to communicate with the spirit world, which comes in from my left. I remain quiet and concentrate on the other side until someone approaches me through my spirit team and passes on information about themselves and their experiences. This information is usually visual, although sometimes the spirit comes through just as a voice. It usually takes only a few seconds for a spirit to come forward, but if it takes longer I talk to my client so that they know why I've gone silent.

When the spirit comes through and we have established a connection, they will want to give me proof for their loved one on earth that they have survived (survival evidence). This often comes in the form of something quite trivial, but personal, and something that I could not have known about, a private joke for example, or a shared memory. It is the knowledge that a loved one is still around – provided by this proof – that gives such comfort to clients.

Often I have three-sided conversations – with the spirit, my spirit team and my client – all at once. Unlike healing, which doesn't draw on my energy, readings can be quite debilitating for me because I not only have to listen intensely but also take on the emotions of the spirit person. This can be especially draining if the spirit passed over through suicide or in other distressing circumstances.

✳

Three years passed comfortably in this way until 1990, when I was poorly again. If it hadn't been for my spiritual medic, Doctor Jim Foster, I wouldn't have known anything was seriously wrong. I had been suffering from bouts of diarrhoea and vomiting over a weekend, which I put down to something I'd eaten that didn't agree with me. On Monday I went to work as usual – I was still working in the Housing Executive at the time – but had only been at my desk for a short while when I heard Jim's voice:

'You need to make an appointment with the surgery.'

'It's a Monday,' I told him. 'There's not much chance they'll fit me in at such short notice.'

But he insisted, repeating, 'You must make an appointment. You must make an appointment,' until, to keep him quiet, I called the surgery and, as it happened, they'd had a cancellation and told me to come straight over.

The GP thought my symptoms suggested appendicitis, but he wasn't sure so he gave me a letter and told me to go to casualty if the pain got any worse. In fact, I wasn't in a great deal of pain at that stage so, despite Jim's continuing remonstrations, I didn't suspect anything was wrong. Appendicitis, I imagined, would be agonising. I went home for lunch with the intention of going back to work in the afternoon, but it was to be six weeks before I would return to my office. After lunch, the pain got worse and my aunt said she would take me to the hospital. In casualty I was examined and a blood sample was taken. They decided to admit me straight away and operate that evening to remove my appendix.

When I arrived on the ward, a surgeon came by to examine me, trailing a bunch of students in his wake. He questioned me about my condition and how I was feeling, and then asked me if I could tell him the colour of my motions.

'I couldn't say, doctor,' I replied.

He thought I was being deliberately awkward and told me not to waste his time.

'Well, I can't answer your question about my motions because I'm blind,' I answered with a laugh. There was a gasp from the students and apparently his face went purple with embarrassment.

'I'm so sorry. These questions are automatic,' the surgeon mumbled and left rather hurriedly. I found the whole episode rather amusing and could imagine the students being able to dine out on the story for some time to come.

The operation was a success, though my recovery was not straightforward. Again, Doctor Foster came to the rescue. I had been put on a drip and the point where it had been inserted in my arm felt a little sore. I hadn't mentioned this to the nurses, but Jim insisted.

'You need to call a nurse to look at the drip,' he directed.

I was reluctant because I couldn't think of a good enough reason to bother the nurse – if I told her I was being advised by a medic who was dead, I would probably have been referred to the psychiatric department.

'It doesn't matter what she thinks,' said Jim. 'Call her. Get her to come *now*.'

Again I demurred.

'You've got a buzzer beside you, press it,' Jim ordered, and I gave in. The nurse examined my arm and said it was fine, but Jim still wouldn't give up.

'Tell her to get a doctor. The drip needs to be taken out immediately, it's tissued.' I could tell by the tone of his voice that the situation was now urgent and so I insisted the nurse find the duty doctor.

After examining my arm, the houseman turned to the nurse in irritation. 'Where did you do your training? You need to go back to the drawing board.' The drip, he said, had to be removed immediately as the vein had collapsed and the fluid was seeping into the tissue. If it were left any longer, it could cause septicaemia.

When the time came for my stitches to be removed, once again

Jim intervened. They weren't ready to come out yet. I suggested to the nurse that it might be too soon but she said the wound was fine. When she tried to remove some of the stitches, a small part of the wound opened. It became infected and I wasn't able to leave hospital until it had cleared up.

My spirit team intervened in another medical situation when I was on holiday in Majorca with my aunts. We had just arrived at the apartment and I had gone to the fridge to get a glass of milk. As I opened the door, I received a shock – of the electrical kind. A shooting pain blazed up my arm and everything went blank.

Afterwards, my aunts told me that before I fell unconscious to the floor, I'd said that I'd nipped my finger in the fridge door. All my muscles went rigid when I fell and my aunts had panicked, rushing to help me. But, apparently, as they were about to touch me I made signs with my hands for them to stay back. Then, my aunts said, they saw me being put into the recovery position and my head being tilted back to open my airway. When I regained consciousness, I was on the floor on my side.

I was unconscious from the moment I hit the floor so couldn't possibly have warned the aunts, and they didn't touch or move me. I was convinced that it was my spiritual medics looking out for me once again. Another remarkable thing was that I had no burns on my skin. The only ill effect I suffered was a tight chest for a couple of hours afterwards and a feeling of coldness from the physical shock of electricity having gone through me. It's amazing what those in the spirit world can do when they have to.

CHAPTER 11

Losing Two Loved Ones

—✱—

My grandfather had moved from home in the late 1980s, while I was at college, to live in a warden-assisted flat for older people. He loved it and managed really well on his own, with my cousin Elizabeth, who lived nearby, helping him with the shopping, and my aunts visiting him frequently or bringing him back to our house for the day.

Having lived with Grandpa since I was a toddler, I had always got on well with him and he was always very protective of me, just like Granny. He loved children and would stop and chat to them whenever he saw them.

I can remember when I was learning to use my white stick how Grandpa would walk behind me to check I was safe as I made my way to the local shop, even though I could do it alone. I'd always sense he was there. 'I know you're following me, Grandpa,' I'd tease him.

My fondest memories of him were when we went on holiday

abroad. He'd be the life and soul of the party, especially after a few drinks. If we went into a bar Grandpa was always the first to get up on stage and sing, usually 'Let the World Go Away' which was one of his favourites.

Grandpa also added the odd dramatic touch to our holidays. We were sitting by the swimming pool one day when Elizabeth, who had gone up to the apartment, shouted down for Grandpa to come quickly. Water was pouring out from under the door into the corridor. That morning he had turned on the tap but nothing had come out because the water was off at the mains. He had forgotten to turn the tap off, and when the water came on again the apartment was flooded.

On another occasion he was trying to open the door of our hired car, and was getting nowhere fast, when up came a customs official. The car, it turned out, belonged to him though it was a similar model to ours. Luckily the man took it in good part, and we teased Grandpa about it all the way back.

✳

I could never imagine my grandfather becoming ill, but none of us can stay fit and healthy forever. His decline was gradual, so he was still able to go on holiday abroad right up to the time he died, in 1995. On one of these holidays he suffered a small stroke but refused to go into hospital, insisting on staying with us. In the end, it was his heart that failed.

I was with him at the hospital the day before he died. He had asked me to give him healing, which I did. Healing doesn't necessarily mean curing – I knew I couldn't do that for Grandpa – but I could ease his pain and make him more comfortable. As I was sending the healing energy I felt instinctively that this would be the last time I'd speak to him or help him. Keeping my thoughts to myself and hoping I was wrong, I carried on with the healing. Sadly, my intuition was right. Grandpa died the next day.

The sense of loss at Grandpa's death seemed far worse than it had been when Granny died in 1979. I was older by now, of course, and Grandpa and I had been together for much longer. My aunts' grief at his passing was profound too, although it was easier for them to accept his death than Granny's because this time they were there when it happened.

The only thing that kept me strong over the funeral period was my knowledge that he would meet Granny and would be happier than he had been towards the end of his life on earth. In fact, I *know* he is happy with Granny now because he has said so through other mediums and also in dreams to me. What also helped me was the knowledge that my healing had eased his pain and given him comfort at the end. He had always been a very independent person, and I think that he had problems coping with getting old.

Grandpa had been aware of my work as a medium, and at first he had been sceptical. With my mother, he attended a Pentecostal church where there wasn't much sympathy for what I did. Like most orthodox religions, the Pentecostal Church was of the opinion that any form of communication with the dead was at best impossible and at worst evil. But I was able to give my grandfather survival evidence about his childhood, people he had known as a child and his own family, information that I couldn't possibly have known otherwise (and which even my aunts didn't know).

This, I sensed, created an inner conflict for him. On the one hand, I had given him information I was not privy to, and on the other his religion dictated that he shouldn't believe in such things. But towards the end of his life he asked me to give him healing and told everyone about the comfort he got from it. In hospital he even told the nursing staff, and joked that he was drumming up business for me.

What my mother and the rest of the family believed never made any difference to me, however. As a practising spiritualist at the time, I had my own convictions and nothing they could have said would have changed them. Still, I am glad that I didn't choose to go and live with my mother when I was fourteen. She wouldn't have been able to influence or change my beliefs and I could never have followed her faith, but I feel that I might not be doing the work I am now if I had taken that path. By contrast, my aunts gave me a great deal of support, and I will always be grateful to them for encouraging me in my work as a medium. They believed I had been given certain gifts and should use them to help people; they always told me it was my life to live how I chose.

*

Many people are confused about the difference between those who practise as mediums and those who are spiritualists. They are not mutually exclusive; you can be both, but equally you can be a medium without being a spiritualist and vice versa. A spiritualist believes that our loved ones who have passed on are always with us, and that this can be proved by survival evidence. A medium is the person who acts as a link between the earth and the spirit world, and can transmit messages of comfort and reassurance to us from our deceased loved ones.

As I've already said, I have never been able to accept the teachings of the Christian churches even though I grew up with them. I was baptised into the Methodist Church, went to a Sunday school run by the Brethren sect, was given a Gospel of St Luke in Braille for good attendance and did an O level in Religious Studies, but I was never really attracted to the ideas and so never absorbed any of the teachings.

This doesn't mean that I condemn religious beliefs or those who follow them – quite the contrary. These days, I practise Buddhism and I respect other faiths and their offshoots, but there has been a massive decline in the numbers of people who follow the orthodox religions, and I can quite see why. As if worrying about what happens when we die isn't enough, some faiths carry with them the prospect of a final judgement, condemning us to heaven or hell depending on how we lived our lives.

I firmly believe we are responsible for our own actions on earth, and that when we die we will, if we wish, meet those of our loved ones and dear friends who have gone before, but we won't be judged by anyone. If we have done bad things and not taken responsibility for them in this life, we will reap the consequences in the next life as we journey through our different levels of spiritual evolution.

I was introduced to Buddhism in 2002 by one of my spirit teachers, Peter. He was Chinese and I had known him briefly on earth when my family fostered his little girl for a short time. He fell asleep at the wheel of his car on the way back from a gambling session and was killed.

I was going through a particularly difficult time when I was living in the Republic, and Peter suggested that I should start chanting. I was rather dubious about whether chanting could change anything in my life, but he argued, sensibly enough, that I had nothing to lose if it didn't work. So Peter taught me a chant and I gave it a try. Every morning and evening I chanted for about ten minutes, and sure enough things began to change for me.

As Buddhists, we have a deep respect for the universe and

everything and everyone around us, believing that we all reincarnate. Chanting is an important route to achieving our goals and our full potential. I chant for the power to help everyone who crosses my path in my daily life and to be able to do and say the things that will support them on their life's journey.

The only conflict between Buddhism and my belief in the spirit world is that I believe it is possible to communicate with those who have passed on, and Buddhists don't.

From time to time, people have suggested that the communication I receive from the spirit world is all fake, or that the messages come from demons and evil spirits masquerading as family or friends who have passed on. I take this rather personally, I'm afraid, because it seems such an insult to the memory of our loved ones. Yet I'm constantly aware of how lucky I am to live in a country and in an era when we are free to talk about such things. No so very long ago I would have been branded a witch for communing with the spirit world and probably have ended up being burnt at the stake for heresy.

✳

At the time he passed on, Grandpa had been going to the same Pentecostal church as my mother, brothers and sister, and there he'd met a group of Pentecostalists who had originally come from Jamaica and were over from England on a visit. As a result, my grandfather's funeral was an extraordinary affair, and some of the more intrusive religious aspects made me deeply uncomfortable. There were two funeral services: one in the crematorium and another at the graveside the next day.

The first service was taken by a Methodist minister who managed to put across the kind of person my grandfather had been extremely well, but the second service bore all the hallmarks of a recruitment campaign. It was taken by one of the group from England on behalf of the Pentecostal Church, and we had to stand by the grave in the freezing cold for more than half an hour, while the group prayed and then invited us to go up to the group leader to be saved. Frankly, by that stage, the only thing I wanted to be saved from was freezing to death. It just didn't seem appropriate that grieving relatives should be given the hard sell at the graveside.

And it didn't stop there. Back at our house after the service, the church group was in the living room with my mother and brothers and I was in the kitchen with my aunts, when suddenly we heard a burst of hymn singing. One of my aunts had to go and explain to them that we didn't celebrate death in quite the same way and that we were in fact in mourning for my grandfather.

All the grief I had been holding back during the funeral welled up inside me and overflowed. Even though I knew Grandpa would be watching over me from the other side, I missed his physical presence and all the happy times we had shared.

I thought of the rose I'd placed in his coffin and the poem my aunt had written for me that was placed with it.

'This rose is given as a gift from me to you,
for all the things you have done for me.
It is given with love and sincerity.
In my heart you'll always be,
A rose for eternity.'

✳

In June the same year, fate struck another blow. My Aunt Hettie passed away. I couldn't believe that another loved one could be snatched away from our family so soon. Hettie, the oldest of my six aunts, had been one of the few people who understood me and knew of the strange things that I had gone through since my childhood. Even though I didn't see a great deal of her, because she wasn't one of the aunts who lived at home, I knew I could call upon her if I needed help and that she understood things on my level. Hettie had been a spiritualist for many years and when I had started my own journey of development we recognised a kindred spirit in each other.

I remember telling her about her grandfather, my great grandfather, David, who had passed on long before I was born. He had been in the merchant navy and had died when Hettie was around six. Apparently, he nicknamed her Bubbles and I was able to reveal this to her as evidence that, although he had passed on, he was still watching over us.

David didn't take an active role in my psychic training, although I feel he might have been among the unseen visitors who invaded my sleep when I was a child. I also knew he was observing me, and there were occasions when I felt his presence more than that of others. There was one time in particular when I knew he was looking on. I was in a swimming pool with my mother, Hettie and my sister. Hettie couldn't swim, and I was holding her hands and swimming across the pool when my sister accidentally splashed us. Hettie let go of me and went under, grabbing me around the neck as she panicked. I submerged with her so she would release me and a pool attendant threw her a life belt. All the while I could see David clearly, watching what was going on. I told Hettie this when we were standing at the edge of the pool later. She said she could sense him too, and I think she felt reassured by his presence.

Hettie was such a live wire. When I was very young she used to wear a coat with a fur collar. I would stroke the fur with my fingers, enjoying its silky softness, and she would tell me it came from two cats, Tiddles and Taddles – 'Tiddles toodles off with Taddles' she would repeat to my childish delight.

Most of my best memories of her, however, were when we were on holiday together or by the seaside gathering cockles and having barbecues and picnics.

One such occasion was the day after my twenty-first birthday. On the birthday itself I'd decided to try alcohol for the first time in my life – I'd never felt inclined to before, but this was after all a significant birthday. My first taste was a bottle of wine called Splendid. It was sparkling and tasted fantastic. After a few glasses of this I thought I'd try something else, some Blue Nun, but the Splendid was definitely better.

The next thing I remember was waking up in bed, not feeling splendid at all. Apparently, Aunt Roberta and my stepdad, Jim, had had to carry me upstairs after I'd passed out at the kitchen table.

The family had arranged a barbecue at the seaside for the following day, and I sat in the car grimly clutching a plastic bag into which I brought up the remains of the Splendid and Blue Nun. Hettie thought it all very entertaining and laughed even harder when I told her I'd never touch alcohol again. This was my first hangover and it took me a few days to get over it properly. Needless to say I've had a few more since then.

We used to have a lot of fun together when we went abroad – the Costa del Sol and Majorca mostly. The only part of those holidays I hated was the travelling. Hettie and her husband were both heavy smokers which meant we had to sit in the smoking section of the plane – I don't think they would have flown at all if there had been a smoking ban on flights then as there is now. However, towards the end of her life, Hettie needed to take oxygen while travelling and I was able to join her at the front of the aircraft, well away from the smoking area.

We must have looked a funny sight shopping on the Costa del Sol, with me pushing my aunt blindly around in her wheelchair, and Hettie directing with her feet and telling me when to stop so she could look at the shelves. But she used to think these were the best shopping trips because I gave her time to browse the items on display. Usually her husband or son would leave her in an aisle, go and get the shopping and come back for her, which meant she had to rely on their choice of items which weren't always what she wanted.

I could understand how frustrating this must have been for her. It's always awkward having to depend on other people for shopping. In my position you never really know whether what is going into the trolley is actually what you've asked for, the right brand of sausages, tea or coffee for example. Not all store staff will make an effort for you, and I often have to repeat myself to make sure I'm getting what I want. Shopping can be extremely tedious for anyone with a disability.

Like my grandfather, Hettie was always very independent – she had worked most of her life. Sadly, smoking was her downfall, leading to the asthma and emphysema that claimed her life in the end. She could have lived longer if she had given up, but she wouldn't stop, and eventually was prescribed a nebuliser and oxygen, which had to be carried around everywhere she went. I feel sure it was a relief for her to leave the physical world; the last few years cannot have been very happy ones for her.

Hettie died in hospital and was buried from our house as her bungalow was too small for a coffin.

By this time, I'd been working as a receptionist in the health service for a couple of years. My employers had only grudgingly granted me compassionate leave for Grandpa's funeral, so I took annual leave from work in order to represent the household at the spiritualist service.

I missed my chats with Hettie but didn't grieve for her because I knew, as she knew, that she had been freed from pain and would meet up with everyone on the other side.

CHAPTER 12

From Stage to Small Screen

———*———

The autumn of 1995 marked another turning point in my life. I was becoming quite well established in the Belfast area as a medium, and the demand for private readings and counselling was growing ever greater and taking up more and more of my personal time. I realised I could no longer cope with both the day job and my psychic work. One of them had to go, and it was the day job. In October that year I became self-employed and devoted myself full time to my mediumship.

Around this time I had been approached by a local documentary maker to see if I might be interested in sharing my story with a wider audience and talking about how I'd become involved with the psychic world, as well as how this other world fitted in with the 'real' world.

The programme, *A Touch on the Blindside*, was to be part of a series investigating the lives of local people and would be aired in the *Home Truths* series on BBC1 Northern Ireland.

It came as a surprise to me that the producers of the programme thought people would be interested in what I was doing. There were any number of psychics and mediums doing the same kind of thing, but according to the programme makers, my story had a unique selling point: I was the only medium practising in Northern Ireland who was blind from birth.

I decided to take up their offer. Knowing the series and its style, I felt confident that it would be a serious and not a sensationalised documentary. It might also help me reach more people. Filming soon got underway.

The programme was to be based on my beliefs about the afterlife and how I used my ability as a medium to help others. As such, it would focus on how I used my abilities in everyday life. One of my aunts was interviewed about my childhood and the experiences I had been having since then, and I was filmed giving group sessions and private readings to strangers who had been picked by the programme makers; naturally, they wanted to test my skills objectively and make sure I had no prior knowledge.

They also interviewed a client about a visit I'd made to his home some while before, when I had described the property as I walked around it with him. The crew went to his house to film the details I had picked up – a stained glass window, a doorway that had been blocked off – things that I couldn't have known about and obviously couldn't see.

Among the most interesting parts of the documentary was live footage of me being taken to the ruin of a monastery that (unbeknownst to me) had been destroyed by the Vikings. All that remained of the building were the outside walls standing in the middle of a field. I had no clues as to where I was, but was able to give a visual description of the plan of the original monastery and other facts about how it had been destroyed.

The hardest thing for me was trying to describe what the attackers looked like. In my mind's eye, I could see men with tall pointed helmets and shields; what I didn't know was who they were or where they had come from, I had to rely on what my spirit team told me.

In the final edit, the film makers used a split screen to compare the original plans of the monastery alongside a diagram of my description. They matched up. This was the best and most dramatic part of the programme as I knew nothing about where I was being taken and had no knowledge of the ruins, what they had been or who had destroyed the building.

The programme also investigated another aspect of my job: rescue work, or getting rid of unwanted spirits (ghosts) in a dwelling. The residents of the house selected by the film crew had heard unexplained noises and complained of a chill in their home, especially in the back bedroom, despite there being central heating in every room, added to which, the place had been flooded twice for no apparent reason. So the unfortunate people had had quite a lot of activity to put up with.

I had handled similar cases before and was confident I could sort it out. My job was to try to communicate with the deceased, explain to them that they had passed over and encourage them to move on and out of the property. But, in this instance, the instigator of the activity had other ideas.

Things seemed to be going smoothly at first. I was in the back bedroom with the camera crew and the owner of the house, and I had encountered the restless spirit who was at the root of the problem. The current occupants of the house were Catholics and the spirit didn't want them in the property, although he hadn't lived there himself and was only related to the previous owners.

I pointed out that since he'd passed on it shouldn't matter to him any more who lived in the house now, but he wasn't having any of it, insisting that the owner, who was with me in the room, would have to leave. Not surprisingly, she refused, so he made his presence felt more forcibly. All of a sudden, she shivered and was pushed forward onto the bed. I could tell how shocked she was – the man, she said, was kicking her in the back.

She wasn't joking; I could see him standing behind her. Placing my hands on her, I asked him to move away and he did. But when she got up to make her way downstairs he grabbed her knee and tried to stop her. My spirit team stepped into the breach, surrounding him, and eventually he gave up and left.

These events were captured on camera, although, of course, what was happening on the spirit side couldn't be seen. I wish it had been possible to transmit these images, not to mention the conversations that I picked up on the spirit side, because the complete picture would have provided astounding evidence of spirit activity.

I have dealt with many cases of this kind, in houses, hotels and bars where there have been unwelcome guests. Usually, the deceased person (or people) makes their presence known in order to attract attention to the fact that they need help. Few of them are evil or aggressive, and in the main they can be helped to move on without too much fuss. This is not always the case though. On a few occasions I have been in physical danger, but I have enough trust in the people who work with me in the spirit world to know I will be safe and protected.

My first experience of a rescue situation was while I was at my brother's new house helping to redecorate the place. I was standing on the stairs stripping wallpaper in the hall when I felt someone trying to push me over. My family noticed me clinging to the wall for support and asked if I was all right, when suddenly my nostrils were filled with the acrid smell of cats and I saw an old lady standing beside me. She was furious about the alterations being made to her home.

I quickly filled my brother in on what was happening but, as usual, he didn't believe me. He didn't believe in ghosts and he didn't believe in my work. Yes, the house had felt unusually cold, he admitted, but he put this down to the fact that they had only moved in a few weeks before.

Reluctantly he agreed to come up to the bedroom with me so I could get rid of the woman. The room was empty apart from a mahogany unit standing in the corner. As I talked to the old lady, the unit started to move forward and would have toppled onto me had my brother not sprung forward to stop it. Then there was a loud bang. He thought someone downstairs had made the noise as a joke, while downstairs the rest of the family thought we had done it. The old lady left the house shortly afterwards.

I got a shock when we questioned the neighbours about the previous owner. According to them, she had died in the house and not been discovered for some time. Meanwhile, her cats had resorted to eating her flesh to survive. My brother's scepticism diminished considerably after that episode.

✳

More recently, I came under attack when I was not on rescue work, simply a guest in a castle. I had been invited to make a return trip to Kinnitty Castle in Ireland, where I had previously impressed the owner with evidence I'd given about the place. He also wanted to take me to visit two other haunted castles in the vicinity, Leap and Charleville. In fact, the area was known as the 'haunted triangle': Leap Castle is in County Tipperary and Charleville and Kinnitty Castles are in County Offaly.

The invitation intrigued me and I went back to Kinnitty, accompanied by my manager, John McStravick, and by a friend from England whose psychic potential I was helping to develop. The 'haunted triangle', I thought, offered an ideal environment for him to practise in.

The second trip to Kinnitty was quite eventful. I was on my way upstairs to my room when a knight in full armour stepped out resolutely in front of me and started to attack me with what I learned afterwards was a mace — a ball covered in spikes on the end of a chain. I could feel the weight of the object as he struck my head and body, and the sensation wasn't at all pleasant.

My attacker, who was in fact English, had lived during a period of invasion and unrest and thought I was trying to prevent him from doing his job of defending the castle. Moreover, he seemed to think my English friend needed protection from me. As I danced around the castle dodging the blows from the mace, my spirit team busily attempted to restrain him. Eventually, I was able to make the knight realise that my English friend didn't need his protection and that the battle between the English and the Irish was long over.

*

Clerics are often invited to perform exorcisms in houses that are haunted, but this doesn't always work. Whatever method they use to exorcise the spirits, blessing the house and so on, is like putting a plaster on a wound that needs stitches. The spirit will almost certainly return at some stage, usually because they haven't realised that they have passed on and are drawn back to a familiar place. Then, when they fail to attract the attention of the living, and can't understand why no one is paying them any attention, they resort to creating a disturbance.

But worryingly, it is sometimes the case that people on the earthly side cause unwanted visitors to enter their homes from the spirit world. Instances of this have increased recently because of the popularity of psychic and spirit communication.

There are television programmes devoted to the subject, indeed, I've featured in some of the serious documentaries myself, but unfortunately there are others that are made purely for entertainment. I have even heard mediums challenging spirits to come through and daring them to cause harm to them. And this I cannot understand. Why invite anyone, living or dead, to try to harm you?

Other mediums have been shown using Ouija boards to communicate, which is especially dangerous because it encourages people without any experience to follow their example. Ouija boards are a tool, but should only be used under properly controlled conditions and preferably by someone who knows what they are doing. The arrangement of the letters of the alphabet and of the numbers should always – and people too often forget this – be accompanied by 'good' and 'evil' markers, and as soon as the glass moves towards 'evil', the session should be stopped. Because Ouija is used by those on earth who actively want to communicate and whose auras are therefore open, it offers a line of communication to spirits on the other side who may seek to cause mischief or simply want to get close to a living but inexperienced soul.

There is also a proliferation of books and online courses on how to develop your psychic abilities, and I wouldn't advocate anyone using these without supervision.

It is far better to learn how to communicate properly with the spirit world and to control one's psychic gifts by attending a local development circle or getting advice from a trained medium.

The problems thrown up by amateur Ouija board users or book-based exercises can be serious, and from time to time I have been called in to deal with the fallout. What is really frustrating is the lack of a support network for the student of psychic exploration – there is no phone number to ring, no place to turn to for answers to questions about the experiences they are having. I wish I had been able to discuss my childhood experiences with someone who could have explained what was going on, but, as I've already said, I think I was supposed to learn directly from the spirit world so that I could teach others more effectively.

My blindness has been a positive factor here. I simply wasn't able to read books on the subject when I was younger. Had I done so, they might have prejudiced me and made me think differently about what I was learning from my teacher and my team. At least I can explain to others why they are able to see auras around people or objects, and why they can see their departed loved ones around them. I can also pass on the knowledge that I have been taught.

When, as mediums, we are developing our psychic abilities it can play havoc with our emotions. This, ideally, is when we need the support of someone who has been through the process and can explain what is going on. The simple explanation is that our senses are heightened and we pick up much more than the average person. As we tune into those around us, we absorb the energy of their emotions and moods, and it can be difficult to cope with this additional burden if one doesn't know what's causing it. We might meet someone for the first time, for example, and feel emotional, anxious or agitated without realising that these are not our own feelings but those of the other person. You really need a spirit guide to teach you about tuning into the auras of other people, and I was very lucky in that respect.

I was once called in by the nurse at college to deal with an incident where a girl had been taken over while experimenting with an Ouija board. When I arrived on the scene she was rolling on the floor in a trance, talking gibberish. I'd only just started on my psychic journey at that time and didn't have a clue how to help her, but my spirit teacher gave me instructions and I followed them. I took the plastic glass the group had been using and visualised a white light going through my hands directly into it. It shattered. Then I placed my hands on the girl and told her to calm down and come back to the room. After a few minutes, she became focused and returned to us. She suffered no ill effects from the trauma but I was drained and shaken. It made me realise how risky using this type of equipment to commune with the other side could be.

This kind of incident is very rare, since we all have a team of people on the other side to protect us, whether we know it or not. I am constantly amazed by the number of mediums who are practising without knowing who their teams are, even though the spirit team plays such an important part in the psychic's development.

Spirit teams are chosen to be compatible with the medium they are working with, and they are equipped with the knowledge and abilities that are most suited to the type of work the medium has chosen to do. A healer, for instance, will have a team of doctors around them who can advise on the best method of healing for the client. Mediums involved in psychic art – those who draw pictures of a client's departed loved ones – will invariably work with artists who have passed on.

The guides are intelligent people who can give advice and suggestions to help the mediums with their development. I am often asked to give details of their spirit guides to those who are starting on the psychic journey, but I usually explain that it is better for the person to try to discover these details for themselves. I know they will be introduced to their team at the right time. If I were to point out that a client's teacher was, say, a Tibetan monk, would the client then try to prove it for themselves and, if so, how? They might just accept what I told them rather than making their own enquiries, which would be a pity.

I have often been asked by sceptics why most of the spirit guides are of oriental or Eastern origin. The answer is simple. These people have been brought up in societies that regard communication with the spirit realms as completely normal. From a young age, they are taught to honour and speak to their ancestors. Western culture does not encourage this. We are a society that tells children who play with imaginary friends that it's all just a fantasy, so children lose the ability to communicate with the spirit world. Perhaps this attitude will change as we evolve.

＊

It had been a year of highs and lows. *A Touch on the Blindside* was broadcast on 17 October and as a result my career moved up a gear. The documentary was a huge boost to my reputation and my confidence in my gift was growing. But 1995 also saw the death of two of my closest family members, and it was my great sorrow that neither Grandpa nor Hettie had lived to see the broadcast. I know they would have been proud of me, Hettie in particular, because she used to joke that she would be my agent. She certainly would have made an excellent job of it, and if I had had Hettie acting on my behalf, the next stages in my life might have been a whole lot happier. But in business matters I had to learn the hard way.

CHAPTER 13

Map Reading

—✳—

The three months that it had taken to shoot the BBC documentary had been wonderful – it felt as if the film was being made about someone else and that I was observing. I still couldn't understand why the public might find it interesting to watch a programme about my life, and to this day I still feel rather hesitant when I am asked to appear on television shows. It is very humbling that people are so fascinated by what I do. We all possess psychic gifts, and it's one of my ambitions to present a television show of my own or make a factual series that addresses this from an educational angle rather than cheapening psychics and their skills, as so many programmes do, by portraying them as some form of entertainment, like a circus.

I wasn't given a preview of *A Touch on the Blindside* and didn't know which parts of the extensive footage would be used, so it was with some trepidation that my aunts and I gathered in the living room for the broadcast. Was this really me on the telly?

I need not have worried. The show was a great success, and the next few weeks were hectic. People from all over Ireland who had seen the programme phoned to congratulate me and say how inspirational the documentary had been. Everyone said how brave I'd been to make the film and that I had come across as very genuine. I was touched by the compliments, as I am by any calls and emails from the public about my work. I reply to them all personally because I want to give something back to those who show me so much affection and support. This feedback is very important to me because it gives me such a wonderful feeling to know that I have helped one more person in however small a way.

Many of the callers following the broadcast wanted to share their own tragedies with me. One woman said she had been in tears while watching the film; her son had been shot by para-militaries in the Troubles and she was greatly comforted by the knowledge that he would continue on and be watching over her on the other side. The woman was a Catholic and had never believed in such things, but she said the film had made her think differently.

The documentary included a scene showing me in a trance while the presenter conducted an interview with a member of my team from the spirit world, the Egyptian warrior queen, Guiveraugh. The viewers could hear the different voice and accent coming from my mouth, and were fascinated by this technique.

＊

Some mediums will go into a light trance when they are working, but the trance state is not a requirement for private readings or public demonstrations so I very rarely use it, though this method is an interesting one.

A medium will go into a trance so that a deceased person can use their body to communicate with those on the earth. The trance state is entirely different from the meditative state, and there are a number of variations, but generally what happens is that the medium has to step outside their physical body temporarily to allow the spirit to take it over. Normally a medium needs to learn how to trance, but I was guided into the technique by my spirit team, and sometimes used it at home to allow the Chief to come through because he liked to chat with one of my aunts.

Even though I am in a trance I am usually aware of what is taking place around me, but I know of other mediums who are not aware of their surroundings, so it is very important to ensure that there are no loud noises. Noise can throw the medium into a state of shock because it can jerk them back into the physical body too quickly.

Inducing a trance without supervision or experience is not recommended as it can be dangerous. We have to have complete trust in the person who will be coming through, and for their part, the spirit communicator has to be trained in order to use the physical body properly.

I can recall an incident at a spiritualist church service when a spirit communicator came too close to a medium and tried to put her in the trance state in order to talk with a woman in the congregation. The medium was one of a group of three on the rostrum that evening and had not been developing her gifts for long. As she started to give the message, her breathing became laboured and she became emotional. The spirit who had come through was the husband of the woman in the congregation, and I could see him standing next to the medium. It looked as if he was trying to step into her physical body, but this wasn't possible as she wasn't in a trance state, in other words, she had not given him permission to use her body in that way.

It happened so quickly that the others on the rostrum were taken by surprise and they didn't know how to react. I quickly moved onto the rostrum, placed my hands on the medium and explained to the husband in spirit that he would have to step back from her. He apologised for what had happened and everything returned to normal.

The trance state is not normally permitted on the rostrum unless the evening has been promoted as such. Even then, only certain church members are allowed to attend because some mediums will go into such a deep trance they will be unaware of their immediate surroundings and any sudden noise could be dangerous for them. An uninformed audience would then pose them a risk.

✳

Shortly after *A Touch on the Blindside* was shown, an Irish magazine, *Woman's Way*, approached me for an interview. The journalist came up with all the usual questions and then asked me if I could pick up information about an area in Dublin from a map. I thought she was joking – how could I read a map when I couldn't see? She apologised hastily when she realised her mistake and explained that she had confused my work with dowsing.

Dowsing is carried out using a pendulum or dowsing rod (usually a forked stick of yew, hazel or ash) to locate objects, water and so on. The dowser picks up the information from the actions of the pendulum and the direction it moves in, tuning into the electromagnetic energies, or the aura, of the object or place.

The pendulum, or rod, is only a tool to focus the dowser. It's the same with other divination tools, such as the tarot cards. When a psychic is giving a reading of the cards, they are actually receiving information from their spirit team as well; they use the pictures and the meaning of the cards to help them interpret the information correctly.

While the journalist and I carried on talking, one of my spirit team suddenly told me to ask her to unfold the map on the floor in front of me – I was as mystified as the journalist. Then I was told to hold my right hand a few inches over the map, which I did, and an image of grass, trees and a park area filled my mind. I could see a road running through the middle of the park with cars driving along it. When I described what I was seeing to the young woman, she checked the position of my hand against the map and confirmed that the image was correct. I was describing Phoenix Park in Dublin (I'd heard of the place but never been there).

I'm convinced that at the time my team were giving me a teach-in, hinting to me about what we could achieve together by transmitting what they were seeing into my mind. It was to prove a skill that would come in very useful in the future with my police work.

I hadn't been involved in helping the police since the incident in Enfield while I was at Hethersett, but things were to change. Shortly after the interview with *Woman's Way*, I heard an item on the local news about a teenager who had gone missing in Belfast on Christmas Eve. He had been seen outside a bar in the centre of town and had then disappeared without trace.

As in Enfield, I started to tune into the boy. And I knew immediately that he was dead. He had got into a fight outside the bar and had been hit on the head; dazed and confused, he had either fallen or been pushed into the River Lagan at a point which had not been properly secured. I could see the images of the boy on my mind screen and, when he fell into the river, feel the chill of the water.

The next day I contacted the police incident room and explained what I had experienced. Detectives came to take a statement from me, thanked me for my time and left. Later that day my aunt drove me to the area where the boy had gone missing and I was able to pick up much more information at the scene. The boy was still present, in the spot where he had fallen into the river, and he was very distressed. He couldn't accept that he had passed on and he was trying to attract the attention of passers-by to help him out of the water, but of course they couldn't hear him.

I gently explained to him that he had left the physical world behind and could get out of the water by himself whenever he wanted. After some persuasion, he climbed out and was taken over to the spirit realms by my team. I was glad I had been able to help the boy pass on properly. His body was recovered a few months later when work was being carried out in the river. In my statement, I had told the police that the body would be found near a bridge and this proved to be correct.

From then on the local police approached me on several occasions to help them solve similar cases. I was usually taken to the crime scene to see if I could piece together exactly what had happened. One case involved a murder that had taken place in Belfast, and I was able to tell the detectives about a footprint which they had missed on the windowsill at the back of the property. This print helped bring the killer to justice.

Police work is not easy or comfortable for me because I have to relive what happened to the victim in order to be able to explain accurately how they were killed. This means that I have a good idea what it feels like to be strangled, stabbed, shot and raped. The sensation is not sustained and lasts for a few minutes only – you learn to control it and shut yourself off from it – and I always feel it's worth the discomfort because my evidence may help to find the criminal.

I also became involved, on a private basis, in helping the families of missing people. They would come to see me for a reading, bringing with them a map of the area where their loved one went missing to see if I could pinpoint a particular spot where they should concentrate their search.

This wasn't always successful as it depended on how long the person had been missing and whether my team could pick up any information. Honesty is always the best policy in these cases. I don't want to give families false hope, so I won't pass on a location unless I am pretty sure I'm correct.

The most recent case I was asked to help with was in 2004 while I was on tour in England. I got a call from a man back in Belfast who lived in a coastal town outside the city. He was co-ordinating the search for a teenage boy who had fallen into the sea by accident, and the search was proving fruitless. Despite being in the middle of a tour, I wanted to try to help in the search so flew back to Belfast where I was met by the family and taken to the area. After reading the map of the coastline, I pointed to a spot opposite where the boy had fallen into the water, but they told me that this had already been searched. Then I was told by my spirit team that the body would not be found by divers but would be delivered up by the sea within a week.

I went back to Belfast and stayed overnight with my friend Mary before catching a plane to Inverness to continue with the next part of the tour. That night I had a strange dream. I was standing in the water with the missing boy; we were talking beside what I took to be a rock but what on closer examination proved to be a sewer pipe.

On the way to the airport I told Mary's son about the dream and asked him to let me know if anything more was mentioned about the incident on the local news. I also phoned a member of the boy's family and asked them to keep me abreast of any news. A week later the family contacted me to say that the boy's body had been found washed up on the beach beside an old sewer pipe.

※

Unfortunately, the police forces in the UK won't admit that they use psychics to help them solve crimes, which I think is a great shame. The police in the United States are much more open about this, and they have many psychic detectives on their books. But then the Americans are more accepting of the paranormal. Even the military in the USA employ people with psychic skills, especially those who can view remotely. Remote viewing is when the psychic travels to a location not in body but in mind, and reports what they can see or sense. It's a procedure I too have carried out from time to time.

Recently, while I was on holiday in Malaga with Aunt Mavis, who now lives in Spain, she introduced me to English neighbours who had expressed an interest in meeting me the next time I was in the country. They asked me a lot of questions about my work, and the subject of remote viewing came up. They were very sceptical about this, so I decided to conduct a little experiment. I asked them to give me the address of their son's property in London. I focused my mind and concentrated on the address. Almost immediately, the image of the house came through and I was able to describe it to them in some detail: the colour of the front door, the layout of the garden, the fact that the house had a basement and that there was a lot of machinery or computer equipment there. The couple (and Aunt Mavis) were dumbfounded because the description was so accurate. It turned out that their son worked in computers.

CHAPTER 14

The Dublin Demonstration

———✳———

In December 1995, not long after the broadcast of my documentary, Margaret, a woman from Kildare in the Irish Republic, travelled north for a sitting with me. Her daughter had been killed in a car crash shortly before. During the session, her daughter came through and gave her mother surprisingly specific and accurate survival evidence. Margaret was so impressed that she called *The Joe Duffy Show* and told the producer about the reading and how comforting it had been. Recorded in Dublin, the show is one of the most popular radio programmes in Ireland and is transmitted all over the country, north and south. The producer was interested and, as a result of Margaret's call, asked if I would go to the studio and be interviewed with her. If I'd had any idea then what this would involve, I wouldn't, perhaps, have agreed quite so quickly.

The interview took place in January 1996. It was my first time live on national radio and the programme had a huge audience, so I was very nervous. The producer dropped a bombshell the moment I walked into the studio: he told me they had phone calls lined up for me to take while I was on air. I asked him to explain.

'Well, you'll be doing live phone readings, Sharon,' he replied.

My mouth went dry and my heart thumped in my chest.

'I've never done phone readings,' I explained.

'Now look what you've got me into,' I muttered silently to my spirit team. When I'd accepted the interview, I'd assumed I would only be talking about how I had been able to provide Margaret with the evidence from her daughter.

However, my spirit team told me not to worry, just to trust them and repeat whatever they told me to say to the callers. I was already imagining what a disaster the programme could turn into.

At the end of the first part of the interview, I was connected to my first call. I will never forget it as long as I live. His name was Frank. But I stopped him in his tracks before he could say anything else because information was already beginning to come through to me. Frank had moved to Ireland from Scotland after the death of his mother, I was told. His mother was pleased that he had become more independent since her passing and moved to Ireland; this, she said, would be a lucrative change of scene for him. My voice was calm and steady, but I was in a turmoil of astonishment at what I was receiving, not to mention fear lest it all went wrong live on radio.

At the other end of the line, Frank was completely nonplussed and asked how I'd known all this. He confirmed everything was correct and admitted that he'd only phoned in to rubbish the whole subject of psychic phenomena. Instead, it had been the best call he had made in his life, Frank said, because he had got so much comfort from it. It seems that once again my team had delivered the goods.

The rest of the programme passed in a blur. I was originally supposed to be on air for twenty minutes, but such was the response from the listeners that the slot was extended for another hour. I was delighted that it had all gone off so well.

I still couldn't understand how my team had been able to pass on such accurate information about the callers to me, not realising then that readings can be given over the phone as efficiently and effectively as at face-to-face sessions. Because voice is my main means of discerning a person's aura and making a connection, the telephone is a near perfect conduit between the client and myself, the medium. When I hear the caller's voice I tune into the energy of the aura and my team on the other side tune into me: it's like a three-way aerial with me, as the medium, in the middle.

If there is a message from the spirit world for the caller I listen to what the deceased person wants to say and simply pass it on. If there is no message for the caller, I will be given guidance for them by one of my team, perhaps about something going on in the person's life at the time or possibly about events in the future. I can also conduct readings via text as it works in much the same way, though in this case I tune into the energy of the sender.

What had seemed to be just a serendipitous opportunity to appear on a radio show had opened up a whole new area of work for me.

When I got back to Belfast, my aunts told me that the phone hadn't stopped ringing — I had given the producer my contact number in case anyone wished to have private readings — and our phone line was tied up for the next six weeks. It was so constantly engaged, that at one point a British Telecom engineer called at the house saying they had received reports of a fault on the line.

I couldn't have coped with all this attention and requests for readings if it hadn't been for the help and support of my aunts. As was the case after the television show, many of the callers wanted to share their own stories of grief or to be given reassurance that their loved ones were around. Others called to book private or telephone readings.

I decided to have another phone line installed so I could free up the main line a little more. I would do the phone readings on my private line and my aunts would take appointments on the other one.

Everything was working smoothly. And then I had a visit from someone who had an interesting proposal to put to me.

Dennis said he had heard the radio interview and he felt I should expand my work to take in public demonstrations in the Republic and abroad – he had, he claimed, contacts in Europe and America. He had thought it all through: the demonstrations could be held in hotels and afterwards I could stay in the area and arrange private sittings. In sum, he offered to become my manager and organise everything for me.

It seemed a perfect idea. For a start, it would mean a regular income, and I would be able to gauge the demand for my work in the south. In addition, I would get to visit parts of Ireland I would never have the chance to go to otherwise. Most importantly, I would be reaching and helping many more people.

My aunts agreed to let me give it a go, providing my mother could travel with me. Mum agreed, pointing out that she wouldn't be actively involved in what I was doing, all she would do was chaperone me and make sure I was paid the correct amount of money at the end of the trip. I had no problems with her taking on the responsibility for working out the figures (my great weakness) and keeping an eye out for me as it meant I could focus all my energy on my work.

✳

Early in 1996, not long before I met Dennis, I had actually held a one-off show in the Shelbourne Hotel in Dublin. The demonstration was linked to the launch of a spiritual society there, which my visit was intended to promote. There are no purpose-built spiritualist churches in the Republic of Ireland, although there are many groups affiliated to UK organisations. It was my first big demonstration. It was also to be my first experience of hostility from the floor, and of being taken advantage of.

I felt really nervous, though I need not have worried. People came from all over Ireland to see me, some 2,000 of them, by car and by coach; so many that there wasn't enough room for everyone. I was overwhelmed by the response. Thankfully, I was able to repay the efforts they had made to get there with some good and detailed survival evidence. On this occasion I was working alongside a psychic artist for the first time; I matched up the artist's pictures with the deceased loved ones of members of the audience and passed messages to them from the other side. The artist and I never spoke to each other during the demonstration but we worked together smoothly as a team. It was an extraordinary experience; obviously I was unable to see what she was drawing, but my spirit team kept me going in the right direction.

The husband of a woman in the audience came through, and showed me a set of playing cards, saying that he had taught her how to play. When I gave her this evidence, the woman became very emotional because her husband had committed suicide. The cards were a crucial piece of evidence; she had placed a set of them in her husband's coffin.

But the team had decided to throw me in at the deep end in more ways than one. When I had finished passing on messages to the audience there was a slot where members of the audience could ask questions about communication and the psychic world. A man in the audience stood up and declared that, as far as he was concerned, the whole show had been a farce. He claimed that the evidence in the journals of the Society for Psychical Research was much more convincing, and that what I had said was too general. Given that this was my first big demonstration and that the evidence had been pretty detailed and accurate, I felt this was rather unfair.

So did the audience, which started to shout him down, saying he was talking rubbish, telling him to sit down and shut up. Despite the attempts of the chairman to restore order, everything started to get a little out of hand, so the chairman asked me to see what I could do. Shaking with nerves, I took the microphone and asked the audience to calm down, pointing out that everyone was entitled to their opinion.

They listened to me and silence fell in the hall. Then I asked the man who had started the rumpus to leave as he was obviously upsetting the audience. He stalked out without another word and I breathed a sigh of relief. A glass of wine was definitely in order before I went out into the auditorium to meet the audience.

Moving among the people gathered there was a very humbling experience for me. They had all hoped to hear from loved ones, and I couldn't deliver messages to more than a few of them. I felt guilty that I hadn't been able to do more for those who hadn't received a message. This was a lesson for me, and I decided then and there that I would never conduct such a large demonstration again.

✳

Mediums who hold large shows tend only to be interested in the commercial side of psychic communication. I prefer to hold several smaller demonstrations in one area over a number of evenings rather than disappoint thousands of people at a single gathering. People are generally entertained by listening to others receiving messages, but if I were in the audience I would feel upset that I had not been acknowledged by my spirit friends. In fact, I am often asked about this when I meet the audience after my shows, and I am quick to reassure them that we are always surrounded by those in spirit who care for and protect us. It's something I always mention from the stage at the end of the shows as well.

There are various reasons why you may not receive a message at a public show. The most common, and logical, is that there is nothing to pass on at that time. If you have no particular problems or concerns in your life, and your spirit friends and family have no reason to worry for you, they may not feel they have anything to contribute. I liken this to making a phone call to a friend. We don't normally phone a friend and hang up after saying hello, there's usually a reason for making the call. Similarly, what would be the point of your loved ones making contact with you unless they had a reason to?

It is also important to go to a demonstration with an open mind. Some people only want to receive a message from a certain person who has passed on, and this doesn't always happen either. It isn't possible for the medium to dial an extension number and call for a particular person. I cannot initiate contact with the other side; I am simply a channel for the spirits; they have to make the contact first. And I am always honest. I will not fabricate or guess anything.

✻

When we pass into the spirit world we need to learn how to communicate with mediums on the earth. If Aunty Flo hasn't mastered this technique, she cannot come through in person, so will send another on her behalf. When I pass away I will have to learn the technique too. People wanting to communicate with us from the spirit realms have to tune into the vibrations of the earth. The vibrations on earth are of a different frequency to those in the spirit world; it's like a musical scale with the earth's vibrations resonating at the lower end and those of the spirit world on the high notes. Spirits have to learn how to bring down the speed of the vibrations to the slower frequencies of the earth so we can hear and see them.

This is why some mediums are better at seeing spirit than hearing them or vice versa, depending on which frequency they are able to pick up most easily. I can tune into the auditory, visual and sensory modes of communication, probably because I am not distracted by having physical sight.

There is no set period of time after a loved one has passed on for them to be able to come through to us, although the minimum is around two months after death. Again this will depend on how quickly they learn to gear down their energy to our level. This is another reason why psychics and mediums have members of their spirit team who specialise in communication techniques. They will have learnt how to control the different frequencies and adjust them accordingly. It isn't as complicated as it sounds but it does require practice and a lot of patience on behalf of the mediums and the spirit teams who work with them.

The fact that most of us on the earth tune into the spirit realms on a subconscious level is another barrier to communication. Those in the spirit realm do not have a subconscious level and therefore need to learn whole new methods of accessing their loved ones on earth.

How many times have we dreamed of meeting a friend or a

loved one who has died? The dream seems so vivid and real, and no wonder. It isn't a dream, nor is it a figment of our imagination. We are in fact meeting with our loved ones at these times. We will usually glimpse these realms when we are relaxed and subconsciously tuned into the spirit realms. This is why our loved ones take the opportunity to appear to us when we are asleep.

※

The rest of that week in Dublin was busy with private readings. I was to be paid a percentage of the profit with the rest going towards funding the launch of the new spiritual society.

Most of the readings were routine, but there was one that stuck in my mind because it moved me deeply. By that stage I didn't think there was anything I could hear that would upset or shock me – I had heard so many tragic stories, both as a medium and as a counsellor.

A couple came for a reading. As soon as I heard the woman's voice I sensed she was grieving. I could feel the pain in her voice, and I did not have to wait long for someone to come through to find out why. Her son, a little boy of twelve, had been killed in a tragic accident not long before. His father ran a part-time paper round, making the deliveries from his car. He had told the lad to sit in the boot and hold on to the papers to make sure they didn't fall out because the boot wouldn't close. It was only to be a short journey, but tragedy struck. Their car was hit from behind by another vehicle and the boy was thrown from his perch into the road. The impact killed him instantly. I knew he wouldn't have suffered.

After giving them messages from the boy, the woman asked me a question I will never forget – 'Can you raise him?' There was hope mingled with the desperation in her voice.

'What do you mean exactly?' I asked her with a sinking heart.

'I thought you could bring my son back. I thought that's what a medium could do.'

I was stunned, and had to explain to her that no one had the power to raise the dead. Her husband apologised, saying that his wife couldn't accept what had happened to the boy and blamed him entirely for the child's death. I hastened to reassure him that their son not only did not blame either of them for what had happened but was with them both, and the couple were comforted by the evidence I had been able to give them.

After they had gone I was overcome with emotion; I felt so sorry for that poor woman. In all my years as a medium and counsellor I had never been confronted with such a theory. I thought of what must have been going through her mind when she came into the room. She would have imagined that I could bring him back to the earth for a little while and that she would be able to touch and hold him one last time. Perhaps she could say goodbye properly and tell him she loved him. She must have been so disappointed. I had to cancel the rest of my appointments that day.

The next day, the woman called to thank me for what I had done for her. I was glad that the sitting had worked for her after all.

At the end of the week in Dublin, and despite the demonstration and all the readings I had carried out, I received very little remuneration. Nor, I learned later, did the spiritual society ever get off the ground. It was a great disappointment to me because of all the hard work. But I wasn't too downcast because the show had in fact been very successful and proved to me that there was a demand for more demonstrations like this in the Republic.

So when Dennis popped up with his ideas for touring the

south, I thought I had been given the perfect opportunity to carry on with this work. All I would have to do was turn up, hold the shows and spend the rest of the week doing sittings. It couldn't be too difficult, could it?

CHAPTER 15

Learning the Hard Way

——✳——

The first booking Dennis arranged for me was in Cork, which set the pattern for the other tours that he organised. My mother and I would arrive by train, usually at the weekend, and Dennis would pick us up and take us to a hotel. Most of the hotels seemed to be unnecessarily expensive and I would have been quite happy in more modest accommodation, but Dennis insisted that I deserved the best because of the amount of work I was putting into the venture.

The first morning would be taken up doing interviews with local press and radio stations, which were pretty tiring as I frequently had to take calls on air. Then, in the evening there would be the public demonstration.

The rest of the week would be spent in private sittings, starting at 9.30 a.m. every day, with half an hour for lunch then back to work until dinner. After dinner, there were more sittings until I finally finished at between 10 p.m. and 10.30 p.m., or on occasions as late as 11 p.m.

This wasn't exactly the relaxing schedule I had hoped for, and the only parts of Ireland I managed to visit were the hotel rooms. I was no stranger to hard work, but this was a punishing routine, and though I never mentioned it to my mother or to Dennis, I was exhausted all the time.

The truth was I had always enjoyed travelling and loved the sense of freedom being on the road gave me. It was exhilarating being away from home, not because I was unhappy there but because at last I could make my own decisions.

My mother tried to persuade me to cut down on the hours, but I insisted I could cope – it wasn't as if I was put under this kind of pressure every week. So I plodded on. I pleaded with Mum not to mention the number of private sittings to my aunts. I didn't like doing this but I didn't want to give up the tours. I was meeting hundreds of people and I loved the buzz I got after the shows. Importantly too, my name was becoming established in the south of Ireland.

With each show, my confidence grew stronger and my psychic skills more acute, but I couldn't go on pretending forever that everything on the organisational front was rosy. Aunt Roberta said I should stop working with Dennis. Of course I knew she was right, but I wasn't going to admit it because I didn't want to stop travelling. The stand-off led to a blazing row.

This was the first time I had stood my ground and challenged my aunt. I knew that she had my best interests at heart and was doing what she felt was best for me. I couldn't have moved out then as I had nowhere to go and I wasn't strong enough to try it.

Though I loved the work, I finally told Dennis I wasn't prepared to continue with him. All the hard work I had put into the tour had come to little from a financial point of view. Dennis's original blandishments turned out to be worthless and, for my part, it had been an expensive mistake.

And yet in other ways it had been worthwhile. Something positive has always come out of even the most negative experiences in my life, and this was no exception. Firstly, Dennis had helped me establish myself in the south of Ireland. I was now much better known than before and I knew there would always be plenty of work there for me in the future. Secondly, I was much more confident in myself and my psychic abilities.

Dennis and I parted company in 1997, and I wasn't sorry. But the argument I'd had with my aunt over Dennis stuck in my mind. What if I did move out? Would I be able to cope?

Up until that point, independence had not been an issue with me, but the experience of my travels had shown me that if it ever came to living on my own, I would never be short of work at least.

In the past, the family had often pointed out that I would never be able to manage on my own because I didn't make any effort to share in the household tasks. I was hardly ever in the house anyway since, from choice, I was working most of the time. However, I had managed in England – after all, we went to Hethersett and the RNC precisely in order to learn how to live independently. The main reason why I didn't pitch in at home was that the kitchen wasn't adapted to a blind person, and whenever Aunt Roberta tried to show me how to do simple tasks she would lose patience with me and do it herself, so I left her to it.

Deep down I knew I should have tried harder to do my bit at home, even if it was just the washing up, and I'm not blaming my family for everything, but sometimes they treated me like a child, telling me I was stupid if I accidentally spilt or dropped something.

Once I had broken the link with Dennis and was back home permanently in Belfast, things gradually returned to normal.

I continued giving readings in person and by phone, and several people asked me if I would consider starting a development group one night a week for people wanting to explore and develop their own psychic potential. I thought this was a great idea and set about finding a room.

A friend of mine owned a house that he had converted into an office to support the administration side of his nursing agency, and, as it was free in the evenings, he said we could use the training room. This was perfect for my purposes and my development group met there every Thursday evening.

Teaching was a change from the routine of readings and counselling, and I loved it. The members of the development group were not only students but became close friends, and one person in particular was my rock. I felt I could trust Richard with anything and that this was another example of the right person coming into my life at the right time.

Richard was also a student who showed real potential as a healer and a psychic, so I often invited him to accompany me as an observer when I went out to other people's houses for readings. Aunt Roberta was not so enthusiastic, nor were my spirit team, but I was convinced he had been sent to help me fulfil my plans.

*

In December 1998 I was invited to do an interview on *The Gerry Ryan Show*, which was recording a programme in Belfast. The show was similar to *The Joe Duffy Show* and just as popular. Aunt Roberta objected because it was so close to Christmas, but I took no notice of her and agreed to do the show.

Gerry is a very experienced presenter, full of banter, and not easily won over. Nevertheless, the interview went brilliantly and he was impressed, saying he respected my straightforward, down-to-earth attitude. When he kindly invited me back on his show on another occasion, my spirit team told me they were going to prove to Gerry that the spirit world existed, but I shrugged it off as a joke – they couldn't provide physical evidence. But that's exactly what they did.

I had just finished talking to a caller on air when Gerry, clearly disconcerted, said: 'I know you won't have noticed this, Sharon, but all the lights in the studio have gone out and the equipment has shut down.' Even the phone system had gone down. Only the microphones were still working. I laughed and told him I was used to equipment acting strangely when I was around, but my spirit team had certainly pulled out all the stops and the results of their efforts won a mention on the Gerry Ryan website.

After the show was broadcast, the phone at home was as busy as when I had been interviewed on *The Joe Duffy Show* in 1996.

That hasn't been the only time my team decided to make their presence felt. More recently, I was doing a regular slot on a late-night radio show in Dublin, giving phone readings over the air, when I heard a mystery voice coming through my earphones. I assumed it was a technical hitch and thought nothing of it until the presenter asked me if I had heard a man's voice. We couldn't catch what had been said, so the presenter asked the listeners to call or text the radio station if they had heard the mysterious voice. We were inundated with calls and texts from people who had picked it up, but no one could decipher what the voice had said. I was just as astonished as everyone else.

After the programme I went into a soundproof booth with one of the engineers to listen to the recording of that part of the programme. Then I realised what the voice had been. It was my talking watch. The spooky thing was that I hadn't pressed the button that activated the speech. My hands had been flat on the

table in full view of the presenter the whole time. The only conclusion I could come to was that my spirit team were up to their
old tricks and wanted to cause another sensation. They certainly
did that.

✳

Some eighteen months before my first slot on *The Gerry Ryan Show*,
in spring 1997, I had developed ulcers in my left eye. They'd started
with a bout of conjunctivitis that failed to go away and steadily
got worse. Sunlight became so painful that I had to wear dark
glasses. Eventually the steroid drops that I had been prescribed
stopped working.

The eye surgeon concluded that my eye was of no further use
to me and recommended its replacement with an artificial eye. I
didn't want to suffer pain in the eye for the rest of my life, so
after talking it through with my family, I decided to go ahead
with the operation and went into hospital in August 1999.

The night before the operation I was frightened and tearful.
Wouldn't an artificial eye be more noticeable than my other eye?
Would I have to take it out to clean it, and if so would it hurt?
My mother drove me to the hospital the next morning and came
in with me as she had to sign the consent form on my behalf, and
then I was left alone in a side ward waiting to go into theatre. I
came round after the operation with my head swathed in pressure
bandages and feeling pretty sick. Once I'd been discharged, my
aunts took over the rather messy business of nursing me, cleaning the wound with saline solution and dressing it four times
a day.

The doctor had warned me that the temporary shell they had
put in the socket until the wound healed might come out of its
own accord when the swelling went down. It did. One night I was

reading a book in the living room when the shell popped out of my eye socket onto my cheek. Unfortunately the hospital hadn't told me or my aunts how to insert it, so off we went to casualty, with me rather queasily holding a hand over the socket and prosthetic shell, only to find when we got there that the horrified nurse refused to touch it. They had to call out an eye specialist, who turned up in evening wear and jewellery and efficiently slipped the shell back into the socket and told me how to reinsert it myself.

Eventually the wound healed, the swelling went down and I was ready to have my eye made and fitted. This involved many trips back and forth to the artificial eye clinic, but it was a fascinating process. First, a plaster mould was taken of the socket; then the mould was used to cast the artificial eye from a special type of wax. This had to be painted to replicate my right eye, right down to the correct match for the veins.

Despite the rocky start, my concerns about the eye were groundless. I have been told that, if anything, the left eye looks more authentic than the right. It's so convincing that people often ask if I have sight in it, since it doesn't move around like my other eye. (I have a condition that causes my eyes to move continuously as they try to focus on objects. But the brain cannot translate what the eye sees into pictures, because the optic nerve, which is responsible for the transmission, doesn't work.)

*

In the last three years of the 1990s, the issues with my aunts were building up a head of steam. One day, at the beginning of 2000, I had finished my afternoon appointments and Aunt Roberta was preparing dinner before I started work again that evening. A friend from my development group came to the door unexpectedly and asked if she could have a few minutes with me. I couldn't refuse her as she had come all the way from the other side of Belfast, and anyway my dinner wasn't ready yet. We went upstairs to my bedroom, which doubled as a consulting room, and we chatted.

After my friend had gone, my aunt and I had another blazing row. She wanted to know what we had been talking about that was so important. I refused to tell her, saying it was confidential and 'none of your business'. She became even more angry at this.

The seed that had taken root in my mind was growing into a tree of certainty. I had done nothing to deserve this anger and I would not be abused like that again. The time had come for me to move out. The problem was how.

The answer came to me in a stroke of inspiration, but the logistics would take a great deal of organising and I would need a lot of help to put my plan into action. Could I confide in anyone in my family? I decided to place my trust in my mother and my sister and told them what I had in mind, although (fortunately as it turned out) not how I was going to go about it. Mum and my sister both encouraged me to go for it. It was an emotional time. Despite the falling out between my aunts and myself, they had always stepped into the breach to care for me when first my grandmother and then Grandpa died, whereas my mother had never really taken an active role in my upbringing. Nevertheless, I spent hours on the phone with my mother when I was alone in my bedroom discussing the turmoil I was going through. I loved my aunts deeply, but I was thirty-five years old and having my independence and my own space was long overdue.

CHAPTER 16

Rollercoaster Ride

——✳——

The decision to leave home was one of the biggest and most difficult I have had to make in my life. It was not only fraught with logistical problems because of my blindness, but the whole issue had become highly charged for me because my desire for independence ran directly contrary to my family's desire to do the best for me by keeping me at home.

In my mind I put together the case for and against the move so I could weigh up the plusses and the minuses as objectively as possible under the circumstances. The scales tipped first one way then the other, according to my mood. But I wasn't entirely without resources to draw on in this dilemma. All the techniques that I had been trained to use in counselling my clients I now turned on myself. Another bonus was my spirit team, and I don't know what I would have done without them. They are friends as well as mentors and I can talk to them any time, not just when I am working, so I was able to pour my heart out to them.

Then there were friends on earth whom I could trust. Richard and a select number of the development group were among these. When I told them what I was planning they rallied round, offering to help me in any way they could. Their support would be essential in helping me move my belongings.

Step one was to find a new home – I had no intention of breaking the news to my family until I had somewhere to go – but it wasn't going to be easy finding somewhere suitable. Among the various obstacles thrown up by my blindness was having to produce my bank account details to a landlord or an estate agent. My bank statements were sent to me in print, so any transaction would show up, visible to all and sundry at home. These are the kind of snags that a sighted person would not have to cope with, which left me with only one alternative. I would have to enlist the help of Social Services. Perhaps they could find me a place. However, there had to be a legitimate reason to involve them and, luckily, since my counselling work had involved many clients in similar situations, I was familiar with the regulations that governed the allocation of accommodation.

Even now, the memory of those days and how I behaved fills me with guilt and sadness. I remember all the good times I shared with my aunts over the years, the encouragement and support they gave me when I first started out as a medium. They had always been there for me, and this was the way I repaid them. I would be so pleased if they could forgive me, and I miss their company, but we haven't had any proper communication since the year 2000.

Yet at the time, I felt there were good reasons for me to strike out for a life of my own. I was, after all, thirty-five years old and had a good job. I no longer wanted to be treated like a child. I was fed up with being told what to do and I resented the daily intrusions into my private and professional life. Despite having my own phone line, which I paid for, I was asked about the calls I got from my students or friends in the development group. Whenever I went shopping with my cousin Elizabeth, the aunts questioned me about how I'd spent my money.

Then there were little things, like the jokes they made when I had to feel for objects with my fingers, such as a cup of tea. 'Are you playing the piano?' they'd tease. This didn't upset me and I usually pretended to find it funny too, but I did wonder how they'd cope if they couldn't see. There was nothing intentionally cruel or malicious, I know, but after a while this kind of family joke gets to you.

The only time I ever argued back was when I'd had a drink, usually on holiday. It gave me courage to tell them how I felt and was a kind of therapy for me.

One of the final straws was when I was questioned about my correspondence. I used to receive tapes from other blind people in England. It was the same as having pen pals but the letters going back and forth were recorded on cassette and we could chat and add music, all much easier than writing in Braille.

So, the scales were tipping towards the cons rather than the pros of staying at home. I never doubted that my aunts loved me and were only trying to do what they thought was best for me, and I could understand and appreciate that they wanted to protect me, but I felt protection was turning into control. I knew the time had come for me to start a new life, so I called my social worker. It was one of the hardest conversations I have ever held in my life.

I am not proud of the next part of this story, and my only defence is that I had no other way of achieving my goal of independence. Because I am not sighted I couldn't move into a hostel while I considered my options. Nor did I feel I could go and live with my mother; we had never been that close, and anyway this would have rather defeated the object of leaving home. And there was no way I felt able to come clean with my aunts and explain that I wanted to find my own place. The truth of the matter was that I didn't have the guts to face them. I knew the aunts would be terribly hurt by what I was about to do.

I told my social worker that I wanted to move away from my family and that I was depressed. I explained how I felt and exaggerated the problems, making things look worse than they really were.

Because of my blindness, I had had a social worker since my early childhood; more recently, she had doubled as a mobility officer. She knew my family history and was also aware that my family were over-protective, so she had no reason to doubt my story. But now I was over eighteen years old she was not allowed to discuss anything I told her with my aunts.

When she suggested getting me and my aunts together to try to come up with a solution, I refused. I had to convince the social worker that this was not a one-off family problem that could be resolved in a counselling session, so I told her that I felt suicidal. This, I knew from the regulations governing the way these threats are handled, she would have to take seriously. She told me to call her and give her regular reports about how things were progressing at home and let her know if I needed to talk, though I imagine she was hoping the situation would resolve itself.

Even though I had put my plan into action, I still didn't really believe it would come off, and there were times when, deep down, I didn't really want it to. When everything was running smoothly at home, things didn't feel so bad. But when the rows started, as they quite often did, I wanted to get out as soon as possible.

I was going through a rollercoaster ride of emotions: excitement at the prospect of starting a new life, fear at the reaction of my family when they found out what I was about to do, and disgust and shame because I had resorted to lying about the people who had brought me up and been there for me in the past.

Meanwhile, the social worker had some positive news for me. There was a possibility that I could move temporarily into accommodation run by the Health Trust until I got a place of my own. I would be there as a respite resident. This was exactly what I had hoped for. It would mean I'd have a base from which I could look for rented accommodation with the help of my friends in the development group.

I was asked to come over to the property to meet the staff and the other residents and get a feel for the place to see if I could fit in. It meant arranging a fictitious group booking so my aunts wouldn't suspect anything. This was easily done as I frequently did afternoon readings, and Richard picked me up and drove me to the residential home where my social worker was waiting with the senior member of staff. They showed me the bedroom where I would be staying if they decided my case was urgent enough to warrant a place. I was also introduced to some of the other residents. They all seemed friendly and I knew I could get on with them. The social worker said she would be in touch as soon as she heard anything.

When Richard and I left the building we went into a nearby Burger King to kill time before he took me back home. We were congratulating ourselves on how well the plan had gone so far when I heard a woman calling out my name. It was my next-door neighbour. I couldn't believe it – just when it looked as if I was going to get away with it, I had been spotted. I pretended not to recognise her voice and ignored her. I didn't want her telling my aunts that she had spotted me because the Burger King was in an entirely different part of Belfast from where I was supposed to be.

When I got back home I acted as if nothing had happened, but on the following morning the neighbour mentioned seeing me – with a man – to Aunt Roberta. My aunt called me out to the back garden where she and our neighbour were talking and confronted me. Thinking on my feet, I decided the best course of action was to deny it and explain everything later to my neighbour so she would understand why I hadn't told the truth.

'You must have got me mixed up. That wasn't me in Burger King yesterday, I was at a group booking in Belfast,' I protested.

'Well, you must have a twin,' my neighbour laughed, but I knew neither of them believed me.

A few days later when my aunts had gone out, I confessed to the neighbour and explained the situation, how I was planning to move away and that it was indeed me she had seen. She promised to keep this to herself, and to give her her due it wasn't until I'd moved away that she repeated this conversation to my aunts. I will always be grateful to her for not breaking my confidence.

A few weeks later, on 20 April 2000, I got a telephone call from my social worker that threw me into a state of complete despair. There were no spaces at the residential home; there had been a delay in moving the woman occupying the room I was to have had into sheltered accommodation. The social worker said she'd let me know when something became available. All my hopes were dashed.

CHAPTER 17

Leaving Home

——✳——

The loss of my place in the residential home came as a devastating blow. Despite the fact that this was likely to be only a temporary delay, I saw it as a door closing on my one opportunity of beginning a new life. It didn't seem to me then as if I would get another chance; all I could think of was that if I didn't make the move soon I would lose the confidence to do it at all. I felt trapped.

I immediately started to feel as if I was sinking into quicksand, with nothing to cling to. When I tried to climb out, I was just sucked deeper in. This was a strange and frightening experience, but I knew from my counselling training what these symptoms meant – depression – and felt even more hopeless at the prospect of having to deal with this on top of everything else.

I slid deeper and deeper into depression. It had been hard enough trying to make plans for moving into the residential home over the phone without being overheard, now I had to pretend to the family that everything was fine when inside I was falling to pieces.

I took to avoiding them. This was easy enough during the rest of that week when I was at work, but in the evenings and at the weekend it was harder, so I spent most of my time in my bedroom listening to music. My friends had always been there for me when I needed their support, but now I felt unable to confide in anyone. I was just too distressed.

My mind was in complete disarray. One moment everything seemed pointless, then the next a sense of relief would wash over me. Home was safe, and the thought of losing its security was frightening. What if my work had dried up? How would I have been able to afford my room at the residential home – more than £700 a month? At least if I ran short of work while I was at home it wouldn't matter so much.

For the first time in my life I was seriously considering ending it all – my exaggerations and lies to the social worker were turning into a self-fulfilling prophecy.

Despite all the people I'd spoken to over the years who had gone through the same experience of depression, I can honestly say that I never really understood what it was like to reach such a low point until that moment. Not only do I now understand why people contemplate suicide but I know only too well the pain they are suffering inside.

✳

During my work as a medium I had communicated with many people who passed on through suicide, most of who were appalled at the pain caused to those left behind. Their own anguish at the time prevented them from understanding this, but afterwards they regretted what they had done when they realised how much grief their action caused their loved ones on earth.

I knew also that if I killed myself I would not be able to meet my loved ones in spirit for a while. When people pass on to the other side prematurely by suicide we may think it's a way out of the situation that drove us to take our life, but it isn't; we still have to deal with the root cause. We also have to deal with the misery of being parted from our loved ones and they, in turn, are left behind to cope with the unanswered question of why we had done such a thing, and couldn't come to them and talk about our problems. When it dawns on us that we have passed on and cannot return to earth to put things right, our spirits need rest and counselling so that we can be taught how to get through this phase.

But such was the depth of my depression that the knowledge I too would have to go through this on the other side did not matter to me.

The urge to end my life had nothing to do with wanting to get away from my family. I loved them deeply, nothing has ever changed that; they loved me too and were trying to protect me. Rather, I was being driven by guilt about lying to those I loved to achieve my goal, depression over my disappointment, and fear about what was going to happen to me.

✳

I knew exactly how to end my life. I knew about drugs and it wasn't difficult to formulate an accurate and fatal combination. The only thing that prevented me from taking this route was the church service I was meant to be leading on Sunday 22 April. I didn't want to let anyone down.

How I managed to carry on working to the end of that week I will never know. Different people deal with depression in different ways. Some people find it hard to concentrate and have to take leave from work to recuperate and get back on track, but I have always found it easier to throw myself into work.

When the service ended that Sunday, I went back to the flat at the back of the church, as was normal for the medium, for a cup of tea with the president of the church. All the emotions I had been holding back – the emotional turmoil, the guilt and the dashed expectations – came pouring out as I broke down. It was the first time I had been able to talk so freely to anyone since the beginning of the whole saga, and it was a great relief.

But it did not lift the depression, and the desire to bring it all to an end was very enticing. When the president realised I wouldn't listen to reason, she was so concerned she wanted to call a doctor, but I needed a miracle not a doctor. I returned home that evening and went to bed early so my family would not see the state I was in.

Then, a few days later, it seemed my prayer for a miracle had been heard. When I got back from my development group the following Thursday, I was asked to go into the kitchen. Gathered there were my mother, a family friend and my aunts. I knew straight away that something was up.

'So, when are you moving out?' Aunt Roberta asked.

I was caught off guard. How had she found out? How long had she known? Not wanting to admit that I had nowhere to go or to appear to waver about whether I'd be going or not, I told her that I hadn't decided on a date yet.

They had caught me out in my deceit and the coolness of my reply must have been the final straw for my aunt, who decided that if I was going, it was better sooner rather than later.

I was worried, but subconsciously this was exactly what I had been waiting for, so there was no point in arguing. Now, my social worker would have to do something for me. I phoned her the next morning and told her I had been given a fortnight to find somewhere else to live. This, I know, was a terrible thing to do because it wasn't really true. My aunt had spoken in anger — she would have given me as long as I needed to find a place.

My call had the desired effect. I was told I could move into the residential home on 5 May.

From this point, a lot of things started to come out in the open. It emerged that my mother and sister had told my aunts of my plans — perhaps my mother thought they might be able to stop me. Apparently the family had found out the address of the residential home and had gone there without me knowing. A member of staff had broken client confidentiality and told them I was to be accepted. Despite my disappointment at my mother's and sister's decision, they had actually done me a favour. Breaking the news to my aunts that I would be leaving was the part I had been most dreading. Now, my mother had done it for me.

Then I found out that Mum and a family friend had followed me from the development group because they thought I might be having a relationship with Richard. I wasn't — we were just friends — but I couldn't understand why it was so important for them to know. I was over eighteen, my relationships were my business and I certainly didn't feel I had to account for myself to anyone.

The only members of my family who stuck by me and were prepared to listen to my side of the story were my cousin Elizabeth and her family, and I will always be grateful to them for that. I am still in contact with them now.

Elizabeth and I have always been close, ever since we were children — more like sisters than cousins. As children we'd go to the sweetshop together and as students we'd gravitate towards one another during the holidays. There are only two years between us and we share similar views about a lot of things. We also listen to the same kind of music, and enjoy shopping together at the weekends and going out for meals.

The weeks leading up to the day of my departure from home were very difficult. I tried to make conversation with my aunts but it wasn't easy for either them or me. My mother and another of my aunts tried to talk me out of leaving, suggesting I might become depressed in the residential home because the other residents were severely disabled. But I couldn't have been more depressed than I was then and resisted their arguments. I had come this far with my plan and I wasn't about to turn back.

I had sacrificed so much to make it happen – their trust and the security of home, things that couldn't now be regained – and I deeply regretted doing it the way I did. But I didn't regret making the break and was determined to see it through to the end.

Friday 5 May dawned, a day I will never forget. Now that the moment had at last come for me to move out, I felt in a daze. Fears about the future welled up and I wished I still had a little longer in the security of my family or that I might have their support if things went wrong. But I was determined to give it my best shot. I would think positive and if things didn't work out I would simply make the best of it. I had made my bed; now I would have to lie in it.

A friend from the development group arranged to come and collect me. It took the best part of the afternoon to pack all my things and carry them downstairs.

My aunts, meanwhile, had gone out, and by the time my friend had come to pick me up they still hadn't returned, somewhat to my relief because I was feeling very emotional. I walked out of the front door of my home, away from the family I had lived with for thirty-five years, and dropped my trusty key through the letterbox, not knowing what might lie in store for me in this new chapter of my new life.

CHAPTER 18

Betrayal

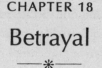

As I climbed the stairs with my luggage to my room at the residential home and then went back downstairs for dinner, I felt as if I was back at college – the communal lounges, dining room, television and quiet room.

Those first few weeks were sad ones for me. My mind kept going back to the happy times I had shared with my aunts, and these memories made me very tearful. I wanted to blame someone for the pain I was going through, and I blamed my mother. Maybe my aunts and I could have worked things out.

Deep down, however, I knew I was only making excuses to help me to deal with my feelings of guilt and shame. There was no way I could ever go back and live at home. My family was not going to figure in my new life, though I was to see my aunts one last time.

There were a few things that I hadn't been able to get into my friend's car on the day of the move and these were still back at home, so I arranged with my friend and her husband to go with me and collect them in a van. The aunts were at home but they stayed in the kitchen and hardly spoke to me. One part of me thought it was better this way – I didn't want further confrontation – another part of me hoped they might have calmed down and that we could talk. Perhaps I could arrange to visit them from time to time.

It soon became apparent that this was not going to happen. And, I learned later, things were made worse when I was leaving. My friend said something and I laughed, which my aunts interpreted as satisfaction at the outcome. They were wrong, but I was too proud to put them right and didn't know how to show them what I was really feeling or how to explain to them that, far from gloating, this trip home had been a very painful experience for me.

As I closed the front door that evening, I realised I would never walk through it again. Too many recriminations lay behind it, and I could hardly blame my aunts for their reaction. I have put that part of my life behind me now and try to live as honestly as possible. 'You can't change the past but you can change the future' is the motto I constantly repeat to myself, but that night, when I got back to my room at the residential home, I cried myself to sleep.

Life had to go on, and I settled into the home and made friends with the other residents. Communal living among adults, who were expected to look after themselves to a certain extent, took a bit of getting used to. I'd been spoilt at home and even at school and college where communal spaces were kept clean and tidy. Here, things were rather different. The communal kitchen and its utensils were dirty. I decided to care take of myself and took the opportunity of a trip to the local shopping centre with a member of staff and some of the other residents to buy a kettle for my room and some other kitchen items for my own use.

There was a wide range of disabilities at the home such as cerebral palsy, visual impairment and paraplegia. At times there were other respite residents who would stay for a few weeks to give their parents or carers a break, some of whom suffered from varying degrees of depression so I quickly put my counselling training to use. But most of the time I was out at work, earning as much as I could to keep up with the expensive rent bill. My readings had to be conducted off the premises, in my clients' houses and sometimes even in their car, because I wasn't allowed to do them in the residential home.

The next six months passed uneventfully. I had invested some money so was able to surrender policies in order to keep up the payments, but my cash was running out fast and I knew I would have to find somewhere cheaper to live.

Although I had fallen out with most of my family, I had managed to make contact again with the youngest of the three aunts I had grown up with. She had moved away from the family home a few years before and was now married with children. It was through her that I had my next stroke of good fortune. She told me about a semi-detached house on a nearby housing estate that was available for rent privately. This seemed ideal and I decided to go for it. I moved in in November 2000. At last I had a space I could really call my own.

My aunt and her husband helped me to unpack all my belongings, and as the house was furnished I didn't need to buy a great deal for it. Social Services gave me a grant for kitchen equipment such as a microwave oven and grill.

I settled happily into my new routine and was soon working from my home giving private sittings. I also started up my psychic development group again. It was great to get together with my friends from the old group, who were delighted that everything had worked out for me, and Richard became a regular visitor, helping me with my administration – filling in forms and paying bills – and reading my mail for me.

Things were at last beginning to go my way. Until one day when I got a call from my bank about my credit card; I had exceeded the limit, they told me. There was obviously some mistake. I hadn't used the card recently, and only used it rarely anyway, usually clearing the bill every month because of the interest. The bank assured me there was no mistake; they had not contacted me immediately as they assumed I would be paying it off as usual.

I couldn't imagine how this had happened, and as I sorted through the transactions credited to my card I became even more confused: the purchases had been made online for computer equipment. I didn't have a computer. I wondered if anyone I knew had been using my credit card without my knowledge, or whether it was an organised fraud. Either way, I was stuck with a debt that came to more than £4,000, a substantial sum of money in anyone's book, but for me it was ruinous. My case was referred to a debt collection company and I paid them a certain amount each month, determined to clear the debt as soon as possible.

Aunt Roberta and my spirit team had warned me to be careful, but I'd chosen to ignore them. I should have been more careful. It was a valuable lesson, but a bitter disappointment, as I wondered who I could trust.

Since then I've had to put measures in place to ensure nothing like this will happen again. I have purchased software for my computer that scans and reads printed material; I receive some of my statements in Braille and I can check them online.

But as far as learning to be more cautious with people is concerned, I had some way to go. Not long after the credit card debacle, I met Ian (not his real name). He joined the development group when it started up again from my new home on the estate, and was looking for work.

One evening he came to pick me up to take me to an appointment; when I got home I realised my purse had gone. Next day I told my aunt what had happened and she asked around the estate to see if a purse had been found. It had, but it was empty. At that stage I had no reason to connect the incident with Ian; I just thought I'd probably dropped the purse while getting into the car.

Later that day Ian came over to my home with his little boy. I was sitting on the sofa when I suddenly felt water being spilled on to my lap. Ian apologised, explaining that his son had spilt his bottle, and I went upstairs to get changed. I don't know why – perhaps it was instinct or I was prompted by my team – but I felt something wasn't right and I took my purse upstairs with me. Having just lost one purse I didn't want to lose another. I left it at the top of the stairs underneath my track-suit jacket. When I went to retrieve it, it had gone.

I asked Ian to look for it because I thought it might have fallen into the hall but he said it wasn't there. This was serious; all my rent money was in the purse, ready to be taken to the bank the next morning, and I grew very concerned and upset. At which point Ian said they had to go and he left without another word.

In a state of panic and distress I rang my aunt and told her what had happened. She came straight round and took me back to her house for the evening. Suddenly I remembered that I'd left my bag in the sitting room, so my aunt asked her son to go and get it for me.

Then I got another shock. My nephew rushed back to my

aunt's house, pale and shaking. He had opened my front door and noticed the lights were on; then he heard the back door slam and, out of the window, saw a figure climbing over the garden fence at the back of my house. It was Ian – and this time he had robbed my safe, which I kept in a cupboard under the stairs. Ian must have watched me opening it without my knowing. He had taken my rent money – several hundred pounds – my Disability Living Allowance book, torn a cheque from the back of my cheque book, and stolen my other purse as well.

Being too frightened to go home in case Ian came back, I stayed on with my aunt for a few days, but I was determined I wasn't going to be frightened away. Meanwhile, Ian tried unsuccessfully to cash my Disability Allowance at the post office, claiming he was my brother collecting on my behalf. But as far as the robbery was concerned, the police said they couldn't prove anything, and I don't think any charges were ever brought against him.

I should perhaps have been warned off Ian earlier by an incident that happened when he was driving me to an appointment. His girlfriend was in the passenger seat of the two-door car, with me in the back, and we were driving along a busy country road. On this particular Saturday morning the conditions were a bit icy, and we were going quite fast. Suddenly there was a screech of brakes and Ian's girlfriend screamed as the car skidded from one side of the road to the other, ploughing through a concrete post and barbed wire fence before coming to rest with its front wheels hanging over the edge of a ditch. Ian and his girlfriend were able to scramble out, but I was stuck in the back with my weight preventing the car from flipping over into the ditch.

I wanted to call the police but Ian wouldn't let me, saying he wasn't insured. Luckily a lorry driver stopped and came over to see if I was all right. It was, he said, a miracle I was alive and uninjured. Then a passing police patrol pulled in to investigate, and between them, the lorry driver and a policeman helped me from the vehicle. I sat in the police car while they spoke to Ian about what had happened. Eventually, a recovery vehicle turned up, pulled the car free and, somewhat shaken, we continued on our way.

If I had known Ian wasn't insured I wouldn't have allowed him to take me anywhere in the first place, but I should have realised sooner that this deceit – his behaviour at the scene of the accident and his ability to wriggle out of any responsibility – were signs that he wasn't to be trusted. He never came near me again after the robbery and I was glad to be rid of him.

It seemed that all my attempts to start a new life were to be thwarted by people I had trusted and who had not just let me down but set out intentionally to take advantage of me. I've never felt sorry for myself about being blind, but I did wonder what I might have done to deserve all this. Surely now my troubles would be over?

Part of my problem was having been raised in a very protective and controlled environment, not being allowed to make decisions for myself and never being exposed to the harsh realities of the real world. I assumed everyone was to be trusted and had yet to learn that everyone is not always what they seem.

Always believing there was a positive side to any negative, I felt that each new experience made me stronger and I was convinced that I would never again fall prey quite so easily to anyone trying to take advantage of me. But I did.

CHAPTER 19

Heading South

——✳——

Finding my house on the estate had filled me with such high hopes, but no matter how hard I tried to pick up the pieces again, the robbery had unsettled me and I started to feel edgy and fearful. About this time I had become friends with a man called Shaun. I had carried out a number of telephone readings for him and we kept in touch regularly over the phone, talking for hours. Shaun lived in the Republic, and realising how unhappy I was, he suggested that I move there to make a fresh start. The home, the fantastic space of my own that I had initially delighted in, now held too many bad memories for me, and moving south sounded like an excellent idea, particularly as I'd been wanting to resume my travels around the Republic.

So, buoyed up with renewed hope that things would work out this time, I took off in June 2001 for the Republic, where I set up home in a property sub-let to me by a friend of Shaun's.

A few days later, this friend informed me that she was moving back in after a row with her boyfriend, only temporarily, until she got another place. I really had no other choice but to agree — her name was on the rent book.

We arranged to share the bills and food. However, it soon became clear that she wasn't keeping her side of the bargain. I'd bought a new freezer when I moved in and kept it stocked up with provisions. She would invite friends round for a drink and cook a meal using the groceries I'd bought. When I challenged her, she reminded me that although I was living in the property, it was her name on the rent book.

It all seemed so familiar. Once again I was having to live by someone else's rules, only this time I was a long way away from friends and family, and there was nothing I could do about it. Trapped and isolated, I had no option but to put up with what was happening and continue my work there.

Shaun saw I was miserable and generously suggested I move into his house just across the street. I took up this offer but shortly after, she finally moved on and I went back to that house. It seemed that I would spend my life moving from place to place, but by this stage I was getting used to it.

The upside was that at last I was able to start touring in Ireland again. I stayed in different towns for a week at a time, holding demonstrations on the first night and doing private sittings for the rest of the time, much as I had done when I worked with Dennis, but this time Shaun was managing me and I stayed in cheaper hotels, and alone. It was an arrangement that suited me. I always went back to the same hotels, where I got to know the hotel staff, and Shaun would call me every morning with the list of appointments for the day. Shaun handled all the transactions and I would give him the money when he came to collect me at the end of my stay.

In November 2002, I was offered the opportunity by a chat show, *The Late, Late Show*, to appear on national television with a friend of mine who was going to talk about near-death experience. It was a fantastic opportunity, but sadly it didn't go as well as I'd hoped. The researcher asked me if I would do a short demonstration of mediumship, and I told her she would need to check with my friend first; he would have to make the decision as I was only appearing along with him as a guest. She said he had no objection.

On the night of the show my friend was given only a few minutes and I was given the biggest slot. This was bad enough, but the presenter didn't give me a chance to answer questions properly and the audience, which turned out to be very sceptical of the demonstration, held back and only reluctantly admitted that the evidence I was giving was correct. This was dispiriting; in addition, my friend was extremely annoyed about his slot and accused me of monopolising the show for my own publicity. We went our separate ways. I only found out afterwards that the researcher had not checked properly with him about my demonstration. Regrettably, my friend didn't believe that I would never have done anything like that to him.

However, I was becoming more established in the south again and everything seemed to be settling down at last. But just as I was thinking I'd made the right decision to move to the Republic after all, an unexpected problem loomed up. In the run-up to Christmas, work began to dry up. People were saving for Christmas and didn't have the money to spend on going to demonstrations or having private readings. As a result my finances were very low. On top of this, Shaun informed me that he was quitting as my manager; the income wasn't regular enough, he said, and the travelling was taking him away from his children.

I knew this was just an excuse. He didn't have to travel very much and when he did he was only away for one night. Meanwhile he had been able to afford to decorate his house from top to bottom. The truth was that he had used me to get back on his feet, and now that I had helped him to achieve this, he no longer needed me.

How many more people were queuing up to use me? How much more disappointment could I take? More importantly, how was I going to manage financially? All this was running through my mind as I prepared for a lonely Christmas. I had Christmas lunch with Shaun and his family and then went home to face the rest of the festivity by myself. Shaun was going away the following day and wouldn't return until after the New Year. Normally he would have ensured I had all the provisions I needed. This time he didn't. I was down to a couple of tins of soup and some tea bags to last me until I went to Belfast on 28 December – I love my cuppa and no matter how difficult things get I never run out of tea bags.

Kind clients, who had become friends, came to the rescue. If they hadn't brought me a hamper of food and lent me enough money for my trip to Belfast I would not have managed.

Once again the right people had stepped in to help at the right time, but the hamper and the money were only stopgaps. My situation was serious. There were no bookings for shows or private readings coming in and I couldn't see how I was going to survive in the south. Not knowing many people there, I couldn't get a replacement for Shaun at such short notice; even if I had, I wouldn't have been able to pay them.

For the second time in my life, I felt that all was lost. If I thought I'd hit rock bottom in 2000, this seemed infinitely worse. I was living in another country. I didn't know anyone and didn't have the support network that I'd had in Belfast. And I could see absolutely no prospects for the future, no way forward and no point in going on. How could I offer myself as a help and comfort to others when I couldn't help myself? With all this going round and round in my head it was as if the walls were caving in on top of me. And I felt so alone. Once again my mind turned to suicide.

I spent Boxing Day sobbing in my living room, my thoughts drifting back to the Christmases I used to love at home with my family while I was growing up. Had there been any in the house, I would have tried to blot out my sorrows with alcohol. I can quite understand how people resort to alcohol and drugs when they are going through any kind of psychological trauma, even if it is only a temporary panacea.

Maybe I was meant to go through this ordeal. This stage in my journey was intended to be a learning experience that would allow me to empathise with the many people I would come across in my work who found themselves in a similar situation.

My only solace, however, was in my favourite music. There were three songs that I played continuously at that time: 'Don't Stop Movin' and 'Reach', both by S Club 7, and 'The Only Way Is Up' by Yazz. For a couple of days these positive lyrics brought me comfort.

I awoke on 27 December with my mind made up. I would go to Belfast as planned the following day, spend the New Year with my friends, then come back to the Republic, take the tablets and end my life. It was as simple as that, my only way out.

I sat on my bed to mix the pills in preparation for the task, a bottle of paracetamol and a bottle of codeine in either hand. I'd never had any trouble opening these bottles before, they were easy: one had arrows that lined up to release the cap, the other had a childproof cap which you have to press down. This time they wouldn't budge. Try as I might I couldn't get the caps off. What was going on?

While I continued to wrestle with them, I suddenly felt my spirit team around me. They told me the bottles could not be opened – they were not going to allow me to carry out my plans. I was outraged. It wasn't up to them to stop me doing anything. I made another effort to force the bottles open, but I still couldn't do it. In the midst of all the turmoil going through my head, the logical part of my mind was trying to work out whether my spirit team could influence physical matter. I had experienced their influence before on electrical equipment, but this was different. This time they were interfering with my will, preventing me from carrying out a decision.

Then I gave my team an ultimatum. 'Here's the deal,' I told them. 'If things haven't changed before 8 January I will end my life and no one on earth or anywhere else is going to stop me.'

I know now that my team were genuinely worried about me as they sought to soothe and assure me that all would be well, that things would work out, but at the time I wasn't convinced. It was just a trick, I thought. They were giving me false hope, trying to take my mind off my plan, and it wasn't going to work. What could possibly happen that might change the mess I was in?

I set off for Belfast as planned, for what I thought would be the last time. My mind was made up; after such a lonely Christmas, I was going to enjoy the New Year celebrations and I wasn't going to spoil it by discussing with my friends the problems I was having. I knew they would try to talk me out of going back there.

The New Year's Eve party was in full swing, the party poppers banged and the streamers floated around me, and I felt so lucky to be among my close friends – Mary and her family – a wonderful memory to hold in my mind while I took the pills.

But then came another turning point. My team had been right all along when they said everything would work out. Someone was about to cross my path who would take a hand in changing my life in a way I could never have envisaged, proving to me that miracles really can happen.

CHAPTER 20

New Beginnings

—✳—

The first day of January 2003 dawned like any other day, but by the time it had drawn to a close a new chapter in my life had begun.

Friends of mine who lived outside Belfast had called earlier in the day to ask if I was prepared to do a last-minute booking. When I arrived at Netta and Brian's that evening, they apologised profusely for asking me to come out at the New Year, and explained that there was someone who was very keen to meet me but would only be in the country for a short time.

I didn't ask any further questions because I prefer to have as little information as possible about my clients, and as he hadn't arrived yet, I carried out a few extra readings for my friends. This at least would keep my mind off my own problems for a while. When, at last, he arrived, he introduced himself as Mark.

'I haven't come here for a reading,' he said, which took me by surprise, because that was what most people came to see me for.

I asked him if he knew anything about the type of work I did. He said that his sister had been for a reading and had been so impressed with my accuracy that he decided to come to see if I could help him.

He explained why he couldn't stay in the country for long, and it emerged that he was Mark Hamilton, the bassist of Northern Ireland rock band, Ash, a group that was so well known in Ireland even I had heard of them.

As I checked Mark's aura I discovered that he was not alone. There were three spirit entities with him. My impression was that they had been with him for some time but I didn't tell Mark any of this, merely questioned him about his general state of health. I asked him casually if he had been having headaches or feeling drained of energy, but I already knew the answer. Yes, he confirmed, he had been suffering from both.

Obviously, I had passed the test by describing his symptoms to him because he then started to open up to me. He had waited for me to tell him what was going on around him because he wanted to see if I was genuine or not. I agreed to do my best to help him, while warning him that we would have to meet regularly and that I'd need to carry out some healing for him. I tried to reassure him and we arranged to meet the following day at my friend Mary's house.

Mark was prepared to try anything at this stage if it would help him get back on track, but I wondered how he was going to react when I explained to him that he was being overshadowed by three spirit entities.

The next day Mark turned up on time at Mary's, and we embarked on our first session. I asked him to tell me in his own words how he was feeling, and he proceeded to describe the constant headaches, lack of energy and feelings of lethargy; despite the medical and psychological tests he had undergone, nothing could be found to explain what was causing his symptoms. He was also experiencing sudden attacks of depression, but there appeared to be no explanation for this either.

While I was giving Mark his first healing treatment, I revealed what I had found: that there were three other people in his auric field and that this intrusion was causing his symptoms and draining his energy. I could only imagine his expression of disbelief and waited for a reaction. Either he would think I was insane and quit the treatment or he would accept my theory.

In fact, he not only seemed to accept this but related an experience he had had in Los Angeles. At one particular gig, he'd been in a dressing room where some people were using an Ouija board. Though he hadn't taken part himself, I felt this was relevant to his condition and I speculated that this might have been where and when these beings had attached themselves to his aura. My spirit team confirmed this.

Looking back, I'm quite surprised that Mark accepted my diagnosis so readily. He is, I was to discover, a very practical and down-to-earth person, a natural sceptic, though possibly more sensitive than he realised.

✳

Auric intrusion occurs when the spirit of someone who has passed on becomes attached to the aura of a living person. It is rare, but can also happen to people who have taken mind-altering drugs, such as LSD, which not only open the auric field but heighten the senses. When the spirit entity picks up that the aura is open, for whatever reason, they take advantage to slip through and attach themselves. Unfortunately, the living person doesn't realise something unusual has happened until the symptoms start.

These can vary in intensity from loss of energy to feelings of paranoia. I am not for one moment suggesting that everyone who experiences these symptoms is suffering from auric intrusion; for most people, they will indicate a medical or psychological condition.

During the healing sessions, my spirit team will try to detach the spirit entity from the aura by weakening them, not by force but with compassion and love. The process can take time and requires patience as I have to act as the physical channel for the work.

Generally, these beings don't realise they are causing a problem for the living person, although there are instances when they know exactly what they're doing and behave like bullies, fully aware that there is nothing the living person can do to stop them.

This was so in Mark's case. One of the entities attached to him had been around Mark longer than the other two and clearly had no intention of leaving. While I was carrying out the healing treatment, he tried to push me away but I am used to that and it didn't frighten me.

There are various reasons why a spirit person might intrude into an aura. In Mark's case, the entities felt they were living through him. However, it can happen by mistake, for example, when people on earth are trying to develop their psychic abilities and their spirit team comes too close, in which case the psychics will feel as if there is a shadow over them. It's extremely rare. The spirits aren't trying to harm them and will withdraw once they realise they are too close, but if psychics are not taught how to protect themselves they can end up in difficulties, which is why I recommend that anyone wishing to develop their skills is supervised at the start of their training.

*

Over the next month Mark's condition improved dramatically. He reported a decrease in the number and severity of the headaches and a marked increase in his energy levels. At first I treated him weekly, then reduced the sessions gradually, and now he is no longer troubled with any major problems. He has also reached a greater depth of understanding about what happened – we have talked at length about the subject since then – and he has lost much of his scepticism about the spirit world.

While I was helping Mark, and because I was concerned to finish his treatment, I couldn't return to the Republic. This meant that my plan to return south, and all that that would entail, was on hold for the time being. In truth, although I was still deeply anxious about my finances, I didn't have time to think about much else. Crucially, I didn't have time to be depressed. It seemed that my team had made sure I wasn't to be leaving the earth quite so soon. Another stage on my journey was about to be revealed to me.

During a healing session I mentioned to Mark that I'd be interested in expanding my work and going over to England – just a throwaway remark made by way of conversation really, or so I thought. The next time he came to Mary's house for a treatment, he asked if I might like to come over to London with him later in January to take part in a documentary.

The film was to be an abstract treatment of the band and its members, and Mark had been so impressed with how I'd helped him that he wanted to include our meeting and the treatment as part of his contribution to the film.

At first I thought he was joking, but it soon became clear that he wasn't, and when he said that all my expenses would be paid, I was sorely tempted to say 'yes' straight away. Not wishing to appear too eager though, I told him I'd let him know the next day.

Deep down I was terribly excited, but I'd already had my fill of people who had given me false hope and promises, so all my instincts warned me to be cautious.

Yet Mark genuinely seemed different; he didn't pressurise me or push me into making a quick decision as had happened before; nor had he anything to gain financially by helping me. The other people I had worked with had only offered to help me because they could make money out of me, but he didn't need me to make money. He simply wanted to see me become established in the United Kingdom because he felt I should be using my gifts more widely, helping other people in the same way that I had helped him.

My team thought this would be a positive move for me, and certainly if they had advised against the idea I would not have gone ahead, but I also wanted to talk it through on a real-life level, so I discussed Mark's proposal with Mary. She felt that it would do me, my confidence, my development and my finances good, pointing out that I'd regret it if I turned the offer down. She was right. What did I have to lose? I had no reason to go back to the Republic. There was no prospect of any bookings there, while England was a big untapped market for me. I called Mark and told him I was happy to accompany him to London for the documentary.

✳

Within the month, we were in London, where Mark took me to his flat where I met Nicky Ibbitson, his girlfriend at that time. Nicky and I took to each other from the start and we have become firm friends, while Mark's flat in West London became a second home for me whenever I was over visiting. I really enjoyed staying with the two of them as we all got on so well, and it was also an opportunity for me to continue the treatments with Mark.

The morning after we arrived, we went to the filming location. This was a building that had formerly been used as an embassy for China and Sierra Leone, but was now rented out as a venue for a variety of functions. The film company had hired the whole building for the occasion, but I was to discover that we were not the only occupants.

To reach the dressing room, we had to go in by the back door and climb a spiral staircase. It was icy cold, which I put down to the age of the building and its lack of regular use, but as I climbed the stairs holding on to Mark's arm, I was suddenly pushed aside and had to grip him tightly to stop myself from falling. He realised something had happened, but I was in a quandary. How could I tell him I'd been pushed by a spirit? Surely he'd think I was doing it for effect. But when I explained what had happened he said he knew I couldn't have faked it because of the expression on my face.

When we got to the dressing room, the other members of Ash were already there with Tav – Steven Taverner – who managed the band, and as I was introduced to them Mark described what had happened on the staircase. I was expecting them to burst out laughing, but they didn't. Apparently, despite all the radiators and large electric heaters in every room, the building proved impossible to heat. In addition, the equipment had been acting strangely: cameras were freezing for no apparent reason; fully charged batteries were running down much faster than normal; and the microphones were picking up static.

I thought I had better explain to the group and the film crew why such strange events might be taking place. We were not alone in the building, I told them, taking care to reassure them that these other beings were not there to interfere with us, they just had not passed on properly. As far as the spirits were concerned we were invading their territory; the two that had tried to push me downstairs were Chinese soldiers who were only doing their job – guarding the premises.

And there were other souls around who had passed on as well. Some of these, I was sure, were in the basement, the only place I couldn't bring myself to visit. I sensed that it had been used as some sort of interrogation centre in the past because a dreadful aura of fear emanated from this part of the building, as if people had been tortured down there. I could pick up the pain and anguish of the victims but had no intention of trying to find out what had gone on or what methods of torture had been used. When the film crew heard about this they wouldn't go down to the basement alone to change or stock up on rolls of film or spare parts for the equipment.

There was a particular segment of the film that was shot in the basement area and I was heartily relieved that I didn't have to go down there to do my bit. However, I was able to communicate with some of the soldiers in other parts of the building and reassure them that we were not there to cause any trouble.

The next morning, the atmosphere in the building was completely transformed. The rooms felt warm and cosy and the camera equipment started to work normally in most of the rooms, apart from the basement. While I was there I continued to work with my spirit team to clear the building and help those who had passed on to move out of the property.

Making the documentary was a real treat and quite different from the television programme I had done about myself in Ireland in 1995. This was on a grander scale, and because Mark and I had to reconstruct our initial meeting and the subsequent healing treatment, it meant more of an acting role for me. I was very nervous, but in the event it went far more smoothly than I had expected. The director told me to act naturally and just pretend the cameras weren't there, which couldn't have been easier as I couldn't see them anyway. Since then I've never found it difficult to appear on camera for television.

The film, *Ash: Love and Destruction*, was previewed in a cinema in London before being shown on Channel 4 in February 2003, and I was invited to the preview along with Nicky, members of the media and a select group of fans. It felt odd to be listening to my part of the film in a cinema environment. But the publicity campaign to launch the film was even stranger.

There were photo shoots and interviews with magazines and the press, and I found myself suddenly catapulted into a completely unfamiliar and zany world. I resolved that the best way forward was to be myself, to speak as frankly and honestly as possible, and this has been my policy ever since in my dealings with the media.

One particular photo shoot sticks in my mind. I was doing an interview with a magazine about my part in the documentary and the photographer wanted to make it look as if there were spirit beings appearing and disappearing around me. She also wanted to make it look natural, so we did the shoot in the middle of Hyde Park. There, she enlisted the help of passers-by, two of whom were visitors from Germany and didn't speak much English. We had some difficulty in making them understand exactly what we wanted them to do, which was to run around me jumping up and down so as to appear as if they were ghosts. I dread to imagine what they thought of us that day, but they seemed to get the idea and they entered into the spirit (no pun intended) of the occasion, jumping and skipping around me while I stood stock still.

Against the background of this media attention, I had been discussing with Tav how I might establish my name in the UK. Much to my surprise and delight, he agreed to become my manager to help me get started. I was thrilled that the manager of a successful band was taking an interest in me and that, like Mark, he felt my work was important. Not only that, but he thought the project would be successful from a commercial point of view because I am the only blind psychic in the whole of Ireland and the United Kingdom.

Nicky, Mark and Tav pulled out all the stops to promote me. Nicky got straight down to emailing television shows and magazines about my work and telling them that I was staying in London and was available for interviews.

I was overwhelmed by the belief they had in me – and hugely grateful for all the time and effort they were putting into helping me.

I had been on the brink of suicide when, it seemed, the right people had at last come into my life, and not a moment too soon. I was determined not to let them down.

In a stroke, my life had been transformed. Everything that I had been through up to that point suddenly seemed worthwhile, and I knew that things were going to be very different from now on. I woke up every morning looking forward to the challenges the day had to offer. I loved being able to make my own decisions about the future and not having to worry about finances. I would be paid for taking part in the documentary film with Ash, and with Nicky to help me with appointments and handling money, I took on private readings in my spare time in London. For the first time in my life, I was truly content.

CHAPTER 21

Launching from the Fringe

———*———

After its life-changing start, January 2003 continued to be a frantic month for me. One of the highlights – although I wasn't convinced of this at the time – was being asked to appear on ITV's popular *This Morning* show. The object of this particular broadcast was to find out whether psychics, or mediums, were genuine or not. My task would be to conduct a pre-recorded reading for a mystery guest, which the presenters would then listen to and judge whether the information I had given was credible or not. (Unfortunately, because of broadcasting regulations, my reading couldn't be played live on air.)

It was arranged that I would be in a room alone with the mystery guest for the reading, to prevent the likelihood of the auras of the camera crew becoming mixed up with any of the information I might receive for the guest. However, when I arrived at the studio I was told that there would have to be a sound technician and a cameraman with us too. This being my first national television appearance, I was rather anxious. The programme team did their best to reassure me, but it was up to me to make a good impression.

I took my place and the guest came into the room and sat down opposite me. I sensed immediately that this was going to be tricky. When I asked him to give me his first name, he refused. This came as a blow, but I decided to carry on anyway and tell him what I was picking up. In front of him I could see notes and paperwork; instinctively I knew that he spent a lot of time listening to people and assessing them. I was also given the name of a very tall woman, Kathleen or Kate.

The guest said he couldn't make sense of anything I had told him so far, so I brought the session to a close and left it up to the presenters to assess how credible I had been when they had listened to the recording.

It turned out that the mystery guest was a psychologist who worked on the programme. I realised that he had not come to the reading with an open mind, and furthermore he had deliberately tried to make it as difficult as possible for me to do the reading.

Hearing the client's voice is very important for me when I am conducting a sitting. I need it to make a connection with the spirit world – the voice is what I work from as a medium. I don't need much more than a simple 'yes' or 'no', but on this occasion the mystery guest refused to talk to me at all and only gave me his name right at the end of the session. It wasn't even as if his name would have given anything away – I don't follow the programme and wouldn't have associated him with it. The cards had been heavily stacked against me, and I was very disappointed with the result of the session.

It was looking as if my first big TV appearance in the UK had ended in disaster. Then came an unexpected twist.

After the presenters had listened to the recording, I returned to the studio to be interviewed along with the psychologist. He pointed out that what I had come up with was very general and didn't prove I had received it by extrasensory means. The presenters, however, disagreed with him. They pointed out that I had been able to tell him about the notes and so on.

Then one of the presenters said she had just been given a message over her earpiece, and her revelation surprised even me. She said that the cameraman could relate to the tall woman I had mentioned. Her name was Kathleen and she was his wife.

In the absence of a name from the mystery guest, my spirits had picked up on a link to someone else in the room.

I was elated at how the interview had turned around in my favour, and everyone congratulated me on it. But my spirit team were the ones who deserved the real credit – once again, they had come through for me.

The day after the ITV show turned out to be exciting on more than one level. Nicky and I were invited to go with Ash to the prestigious NME music awards ceremony, and along with all the famous people who attended the awards, I had to walk up the press aisle outside the venue between the banks of journalists and popping cameras. A few journalists called out to me to say how well I had done the previous day on *This Morning* and asked for interviews. I was a bit nonplussed, though proud, that even in the presence of other celebrities, the journalists had taken notice of the programme and knew who I was.

After a scrumptious meal, the ceremony got under way and one by one the musicians and lyricists went up to the podium to receive their awards. During the presentations, however, I became aware that there were other beings in the room quite apart from the invited guests. The Clash were being presented with an award and one of the group was saying how proud Joe Strummer would have been had he been there to receive the award along with the rest of the band.

Suddenly, I heard a voice in my ear and saw a man pointing up at the stage, guffawing at this speech. He told me to tell the guy to stop waffling and get off the stage. With a shock I realised it was Joe Strummer himself who was talking to me.

I leaned over and told Mark and Tav what was happening. That, they said, was exactly what Joe's reaction would have been, and when I described the spirit to Tav he confirmed that it had to be Joe. Although I had heard of the legendary punk band, I hadn't realised that Joe had died. Since then I have met his wife and been able to give her personal information from him that she says has been a great comfort to her.

Although the Ash film had generated some media interest in me and I had appeared on *This Morning*, I still needed a plan of action to get my name known more widely in the UK.

Tav and I discussed various ways I might attract media attention in my own right but to start with we drew a blank, so he decided to enlist the help of a public relations consultant who might have some ideas from a PR angle. When we met she asked me about my work and my goals. I told her everything I had done in Ireland and how successful my shows had been there, and how much I wanted to repeat the experience in the UK so that I could use my gifts to help more people.

She came up with the idea of using the Edinburgh Festival as a launch pad for me. I'd heard of the festival, of course, but didn't really know what happened there or how famous it was world-wide — which was probably just as well, because had I realised what lay ahead I might never have agreed to do it, and that would certainly have been a mistake.

We thought that I should try for a slot on the Edinburgh Fringe Festival in August 2003. The Fringe, as the name suggests, is a part of the festival on the periphery of the main events, less structured but a big draw, and a good platform for comedy, satire, and more off-beat theatre and music. I was to have a show in a new venue called the Pod Theatre, a marquee constructed to look like a proper theatre inside and with seats arranged in a circle around the stage. My show, Second Sight, was to run for an hour in the afternoon, from 3 p.m. to 4 p.m., seven days a week throughout August.

I spent the months in the run-up to the festival travelling between England and Belfast to promote the event. There were countless interviews with the press and photo shoots for the PR launch. It was exhausting but exciting, and so frenetic that I often felt detached from all the publicity, as if I was observing everything that was happening from the outside. There were days when I had to give four or five interviews in a row, always answering the same questions. 'How did you find out you had such an amazing gift?' 'When did you start using it to help people?' – I became quite proficient in interview techniques. Some of the journalists wanted me to do readings for them as well, so they could report on how accurate I had been.

It was only at this point that I realised what a high profile the festival had, and worried that my spirit team had thrown me in at the deep end again. But they seemed confident enough that I could handle the shows and the media pressure, and I trusted them completely. It still didn't stop me from being rather anxious. Not only did the festival attract media from all over the world, but it was a huge draw for celebrities as well.

*

I have since learned that celebrities are just like everyone else and meeting them has long ceased to bother me. Thanks to the contacts I made through Ash, I went on to carry out a number of readings for television presenters, actors and members of well-known bands, including The Cranberries, Melinda Messenger, James Nesbitt and Janet Ellis. My approach is simply to treat them all as human beings who have feelings and problems like the rest of us, which is after all exactly what they are. They have the same worries as everyone else and they know I would never divulge what we discuss during the readings.

Respect for client confidentiality is absolutely essential, but sadly there have been psychics who have written about celebrity readings, and this, I feel, is completely unethical unless express permission has been granted. A medium should seek recognition through their own achievements rather than use the status of others to further their career.

✳

Finally, August arrived and I set off for Edinburgh, eagerly looking forward to the challenge but with little idea of exactly what that challenge might be.

My Belfast friend, Mary, had asked her father, John, to go with me, which he kindly agreed to do as he had a few weeks free. I had met John, through Mary, in 2000 but this was the first time we had worked together. He was another sceptic, but soon changed his opinion after witnessing the evidence I was able to give at the shows in Edinburgh. John is now my manager and has been my rock over the past three years. I don't know what I would do without him. His advice is blunt but sound, and he has always been ready with words of encouragement when I need a lift. We have an excellent working relationship and I would trust him with my life.

The first week of Second Sight at The Pod was the most nerve-wracking of my career. The demonstrations were arranged primarily for the press so they could run features on them, and a few celebrities came along as well. These shows were particularly tricky because the people who came to them weren't 'natural' audiences for a medium.

✳

Demonstrations are not like readings. When I am doing a show I need to have a good rapport with the audience in order to make it work. I don't want them to give me any information but I do need them to speak to me. One reason is because I can't see where they are sitting so cannot face the person properly unless I can hear them. But the main reason is that I need to hear the person's voice so as to make a connection between them and their loved one who has passed on. I always explain to the audience that I am the channel between the earth and the spirit world and I can hear their loved ones speaking to me as if on a physical level, but I can only communicate with whoever communicates with me and I can only pass on what I am given.

The show flows really well when the members of the audience react to me and work with me, but if they simply nod in agreement or don't acknowledge me at all, which is effectively what happened with the press and celebrities in Edinburgh, it can be a frustrating experience not only for me but for the spirit people who are trying to communicate. I cannot see a nod, and if no one is prepared to accept a message, the communication cannot go any further. I can't count the times that a member of an audience has sidled up to me after a show and told me they understood everything I was saying but didn't speak up because they were too shy.

It is so important to be aware that when you attend a mediumistic demonstration, you might be picked from the audience to receive a message from the spirit world. I do not choose who I speak to. If your family or friends want to communicate with you they will seize the opportunity while they can, so, if you have come this far, you mustn't be shy, you must be ready to speak up if you are addressed from the stage. Nor is there anything to fear. Your loved ones will not say anything to alarm or frighten you.

A lot of people worry that their personal business will be revealed from the stage, but this doesn't happen. If I am given information of a sensitive nature I will ask the recipient to come and speak to me after the show. Another myth is that you will hear bad news. This is not true either. Those on the other side are mostly only interested in giving survival evidence to prove to you, their loved one, that they actually can communicate, so they are not likely to say anything to upset you. The message they will send usually contains information that is known only to the sender and the recipient.

Audiences need to realise, too, that spirits only give the information they want to give and the medium doesn't always get the whole picture.

✳

In Edinburgh I was performing in front of an audience who were there mainly to be entertained – that is what the Edinburgh Festival and Fringe are all about – and the majority of people visiting the Fringe are regulars. My Second Sight show was different from the usual mix of comedy and music on the Fringe. Added to which, it was staged in the afternoon when most of the other entertainments were closed, and a lot of people came for want of anything else to do. There were days when I found it difficult to capture and hold their attention.

Only a few of the ticket holders came in the hope of hearing from their loved ones in the spirit world. When I am on tour, the audiences are largely made up of people who have chosen, and paid, to come to the shows to see me. They are there in the hope of receiving a message of comfort or evidence that their loved ones are still around.

The festival was a steep learning curve for me, the first big event I had done in the UK, and I wasn't as confident on stage as I am now. Faced with such problems these days, I would have less trouble dealing with them because my tours have given me experience of such a wide variety of audiences.

There was also the weather to contend with in Edinburgh. Britain was in the middle of a heat wave in the summer of 2003, and I fried under the stage lights. It wouldn't have been so bad had the theatre been in a traditional building, but the marquee was stifling and the theatre staff completely unprepared for the tropical temperatures. For the first week there was no air conditioning, and I stood on stage dripping with nerves and the heat, with John standing by with bottles of cold water for when I felt faint or dizzy. When things were particularly difficult I fancied I could hear my grandmother spurring me on.

Despite all this, the shows were always well attended and most of the reviews were enthusiastic. One journalist even included Second Sight in his list of ten things to do on the Fringe, recommending in his article that people come and see the show.

My confidence grew gradually with every show, and so did my own enjoyment, especially the rush of adrenalin when the show was over and the audience was satisfied. I didn't need to be able to see their faces to know if they had enjoyed the experience or not. I could tune into the energy in the room. If the auras looked opened up and the vibrations blended together then the people were happy; if their auras were closed up then they hadn't enjoyed themselves. And some people, if they came to a show merely to be entertained, didn't always enjoy themselves.

Not surprisingly, people responded most enthusiastically to messages that were either amusing or emotionally charged. At one show, I gave a message to a woman from her father who had passed on. He asked me to pass on to her a teasing reminder about being afraid of the dark, especially on the Tube in London. She laughed and explained to the rest of the audience that when she was twelve years old, she had been on a Tube train that had stopped working in the middle of a tunnel, plunging the carriage into darkness. This had become a personal joke between her and her father, something that was known only to the two of them.

On another occasion a more dramatic story lay behind the message I passed on to a young girl in the audience from her boyfriend in the spirit world. The couple had been engaged to be married and I was able to describe what the girl's engagement ring looked like. Then I saw the colour red, at which point I stopped and told the girl I was getting something that was very personal.

At first I couldn't work out what this meant, then I realised that there was blood everywhere. The boy had been in the RAF and had been court marshalled for some offence. Unable to stand the stigma of it, he had shot himself and the walls of his room at the base were covered with his blood. I was able to convey the gist of the matter in public but I didn't reveal the detail. In his message to his girl, he tenderly encouraged her to stop grieving for him, to move on now and be happy — he would be looking after her. It was one of the few shows where there wasn't a dry eye in the house. Afterwards the girl came up and thanked me. It was, she said, the best message she had ever received from him.

Sometimes a spirit will come through because he or she wants to explain exactly what happened to them when they passed over. At one show in Edinburgh, for example, I received a message from a man who had drowned at sea. At first no one accepted the message.

'It didn't happen in a boat, and it wasn't exactly an accident,' I was able to elaborate. When a member of the audience accepted the message I was able to tell them how the man had died. He was escaping from an oil rig that had caught fire, and at first I sensed that he had hit his head on a rock under the water, but he told me the object wasn't a rock, it was the concrete leg of the rig.

✳

Apart from the shows on the Fringe, I was still required to do interviews and photo shoots for the press. One in particular stands out for me as it was held late at night in an unusual venue – a graveyard. The feature was for a Sunday supplement but the scenario would have looked good in a Halloween horror movie. I had to stand beside a headstone and a Celtic cross in the oldest graveyard in Edinburgh. Dressed completely in white because I still wearing my stage clothes, I must have looked as if I was about to perform a magical ritual. I was extremely relieved when the shoot was over.

Visiting cemeteries is an anathema to me. I am constantly bombarded with messages from the people who have passed on. They know I can hear and talk to them and will crowd around, badgering me to give messages to their loved ones who are visiting the graves. Not only that, but a cemetery is also a place of grief and pain, which I pick up from the mourners and experience keenly with them. All this creates a dilemma for me. It would not be respectful or appropriate for me to approach someone in the middle of their grief with survival evidence; at the same time, the spirits of the departed are bursting with the desire to comfort their loved ones. My heart goes out to the mourners. If only I could convey these messages and feelings to them without the need to use physical speech. It would be wonderful to be able to reassure them that their family and friends are happy and watching over them.

CHAPTER 22

My Beautiful Career

—✳—

By the time the Edinburgh Festival drew to a close, I was exhausted but exhilarated. However, I wasn't allowed to put my feet up for long. Tav had come up with the idea of capitalising on the publicity I'd received on the Fringe by taking the Second Sight show on the road, and within two months I was off round England and Scotland on a forty-eight-venue tour.

There have been four Second Sight tours to date and, thanks to Tav, we came up with a format that worked from the start. Although I had done demonstrations before across Ireland, these had no real shape to them. Second Sight not only introduced a proper structure to the proceedings, but the experience in Edinburgh taught me how to conduct myself on stage, deliver messages effectively and manage a sceptical or hostile audience. Sadly, my professional relationship with Tav was not open-ended. Having got me off to such a fantastic start and set me on the right road, he needed to get back to managing Ash. For a short while, Second Sight management was taken over by Richard Griffith until John, then my Irish manager, took over for the second tour. Now John manages both the UK and Ireland for me, organising meetings, accommodation and transport. Once at the venue, John organises sound and camera checks and makes sure the 'runners' (staff who take the microphone to people in the audience) have their instructions.

The shows open with a pre-recorded sound introduction, which Tav devised and recorded in his splendidly clear and authoritative voice. This aims to let the audience know what to expect from the show and how it will be conducted. It explains that I am not a fortune teller but a channel for the spirit world. It also asks that when I am speaking to a member of the audience they answer me directly rather than give me non-verbal signals, such as nods, shakes of the head, shrugs, as I can't see these. Finally, Tav explains that the person to whom I am communicating should give me their first name, but apart from that must only answer 'yes' or 'no'.

The introduction was specifically designed for a general Edinburgh Festival audience but we've used it ever since because it means I can focus for most of the show on giving as much survival evidence as possible.

During the show, I stand the whole time on stage in front of a fixed microphone – I don't want to risk falling off and, anyway, I have a video camera trained on me so that my face is on the screen the whole time; a roving camera projects onto a screen a picture of the person who is receiving the message. That way everyone in the room can see what is going on and feel involved. Watching the reactions of a recipient can be almost as rewarding for the audience as being given a message themselves.

When a spirit comes through to me with an image or snippet

of information, I will give this to the audience and hope someone will understand. If no one picks up on the message immediately, I will try to narrow it down. The spirit might give me a name,
for instance Anne or Margaret, of whom there may be several in
the audience. Once I hear a voice, I can try to establish which
Anne or Margaret it is. During one demonstration in Glasgow,
a spirit wanted to communicate with one of three sisters in the
audience, identifying her as 'the one who inherited her mother's
blue and cream tea set', and then, to the great delight of the audience, adding, 'You never liked it, did you? You threw it in the bin.'

Demonstrations can turn very tense and emotional. This is
especially true for those who have lost a child. I have often been
asked to let the parent of a dead child know that the child is
happy and being looked after by a relative on the other side. If
the child has passed on through an accident or, for example, a cot
death, they will ask me to reassure their mother or father that it
was not their fault and they should not feel guilty about the
circumstances. Sometimes, the child will simply ask me to say
goodbye to their loved ones.

I recall an incident that happened during one of my Second
Sight shows in Worthing and indeed featured in the local paper
the following day. A message came through from a little girl who
had died from natural causes as a baby. She asked me to let her
mum know she was happy and was being looked after by her nan.
Then she thanked her mum for spreading the rose petals over her
memory place.

This was a particularly moving communication, and I had difficulty holding back the tears as I delivered the message with its
words of love and tenderness from the little girl to her mother.
The woman stood up in front of the audience and explained that
she had made a small shrine to her daughter in the room she had

used as a nursery. Every morning she would buy a bunch of roses and sprinkle the fresh rose petals over the room. It was a privilege for me to be able to bring such comfort to the grieving mother.

Sadly, I can only get around a certain number of people in one evening, so I always reassure those who have not had a message that it doesn't mean their loved ones are not around or that they don't wish to talk to them.

Even with the taped explanation, it is difficult sometimes for people to take fully on board what is happening. Misunderstandings are not unusual. On one tour, I had a message from the father of an elderly lady in the audience.

'It can't be my father!' she exclaimed. 'He's been dead for years.'

'Well, I should hope so,' I said with some amusement, and the lady, who had apparently looked petrified at first, suddenly realised her mistake and joined in the audience's laughter.

When the demonstration has finished I take time to meet the audience and chat to them, so I can show my appreciation of their support and answer any questions they may have. I usually have to make it clear that I cannot conduct readings on the spot since they take time and a lot of energy, but I give my contact details to anyone who is interested so they can make a private appointment if they wish.

*

One of the joys of touring is visiting so many places across the UK and Ireland. Often it is the venue itself that is memorable because of the ghosts I've encountered who inhabit them.

I usually arrive early to allow time for the audio-visual crew to set up their equipment before the show starts. At a venue in Gravesend in Kent in 2005, I was killing time in my dressing room when a woman's voice broke through my thoughts. She asked me if I wanted anything and if I was OK. At first I assumed it was one of the staff, but the door hadn't opened or I would have heard it. Then I saw her: a short, plump woman dressed in a nurse's uniform stood in front of me with a small torch in her hand. It was the kind of torch nurses use when they are doing the rounds at night so as not to disturb the patients. I told her I was fine and that I didn't need anything and thanked her for her concern. She disappeared.

When I went on stage I described what had happened in the dressing room to the audience. After the show I got chatting with one of the older members of staff at the theatre, and she explained that it had been built on the foundations of an old sanatorium. This had been used as an isolation hospital during the Second World War to treat wounded soldiers brought from the ships that docked in the town.

A few weeks later an article appeared in the local Gravesend press. A man who used to work at the theatre had been in the audience the night of my show and had heard my story about the nurse with interest. He had also seen her when he was working there but he had never mentioned it to anyone in case they thought he was mad. At last he felt able to break his silence.

I had a similar experience while I was performing in a theatre in the north of England. As I was walking into the building on my way to the dressing room, I saw a man dressed in a grey suit standing by the stage. Without thinking, I asked the member of staff with me who the man was, but my companion couldn't see anyone. Whoever it was followed me to the dressing room and told me that he had been the caretaker when the building was a lace-making factory.

On my way back to the auditorium with my staff minder

before the show started, I pointed out a part of the wall that had been blocked up where once there had been a spiral staircase. It seemed the man who had passed on was trying to find his old room and couldn't because the staircase had been removed – this was confirmed by the staff who worked at the venue.

After the show, I told the old caretaker that the staircase wasn't there any longer and he didn't have to stay in the building, but he wanted to know who would take over his job if he left. I had to explain that his job no longer existed, but at least I was able to reassure him that he could rest.

Apparently, the man had been seen before and was rumoured to be searching for his dog, though we now know this was not the case. Other mediums had performed at that venue, but I was the only one to have sensed the ghost of the caretaker.

During a more recent tour, I was asked to visit the military base in Aldershot where the librarian had reported some ghostly activity in the library. There were a few journalists there and a presenter from the base's radio station who wanted to record anything that happened for airing later. When we arrived in Aldershot, snow lay on the ground and it was freezing, so we went into the library for a cup of tea before I started my investigation. As I sat down I heard the sound of someone doing a very bad job of tuning the bagpipes. I assumed there was a practice session going on in one of the rooms adjoining the library and didn't mention it.

When I was ready, the librarian took me through the library. At first I didn't sense anything unusual and was rather disappointed because I knew I would have to tell the journalists that I'd drawn a blank. Then I heard the bagpipes again and joked to the librarian that whoever was trying to tune them shouldn't give up their day job.

'I'm sorry,' she said. 'What bagpipes?'

'The ones we heard in the music rooms when I first arrived,' I replied.

'There aren't any music rooms in this part of the building,' she said, with a note of surprise in her voice.

So, I was sensing something after all. Then I smelt a sweet fragrance – flowers, but flowers of the kind you would find in the Far East (I don't know why that thought suddenly came into my head as I've never been there). Then the perfume swiftly changed to the smell of tobacco smoke, as if someone had lit a pipe. I relayed all this information to the others.

There was someone else in the library quite apart from us physical beings, and I knew that the paranormal activity had been created to attract my attention to their presence. His name was Robert. He told me he had been discharged from the army on medical grounds with shell shock, and used to visit the library on a regular basis after his discharge. The librarian confirmed that she had smelt the tropical fragrance and the tobacco, but had never heard the bagpipes.

Robert was determined to prove who he was. 'I want you to find a book for me,' he told me. 'It's there, on the trolley.'

'What trolley?' I asked. I knew the walls of the library were covered in books, but Robert said there was a trolley standing in the middle of the floor. I was nervous about following the instructions of a stranger I wasn't sure I could trust in the presence of the media, but I took a chance and asked the librarian to take me over to the trolley.

'It's on the bottom shelf. Leaf through it and I'll tell you where to stop,' said Robert directing my hand to the volume.

The book was a guide to the names and uniforms of British regiments, and I turned the pages as directed until he stopped me on a page that showed a soldier in the uniform of a Highland regiment. Everyone in the room, including me, was astonished. How could I have known where the book was, never mind the page that showed the uniform?

It transpired that Robert was perfectly happy residing in the library and, as he hadn't caused any trouble and the staff were now aware of him, we decided not to move him on. Robert has adjusted to the fact that he has died, and while he doesn't stay in the library all the time, he visits whenever he wants. I just hope Robert doesn't make a regular habit of playing the bagpipes.

The next day I got a call from the radio station asking me for a telephone interview. The recording of the events in the library had been ruined by static. Once again this came as no surprise to me, though it was a great pity the recording had been lost.

CHAPTER 23

TV Highs and Lows

—*—

As a media launch pad for me, the Edinburgh Fringe began to pay off almost immediately. I made a number of television appearances, among them *The Salon* on Channel 4, *LK Today* (Lorraine Kelly) and *Loose Lips* on UK Living, and my story featured in several popular magazines such as *Chat* and *Now*. But perhaps the most prestigious approach came, while I was still in Edinburgh, from the Religion and Ethics Department of the BBC. They asked if I would like to take part in a documentary for its *Everyman* television series that would observe three well-known mediums as they went about their work, at home and on tour. They had chosen me as one of the mediums because of the positive reviews for Second Sight coming out of The Fringe. The fact that I was blind was of added interest to them because, as they explained, it would give the programme a different slant.

This was an opportunity I wasn't going to miss – *Everyman* was such a highly respected series – and an important step along the way in my career in the UK. A film crew came over to Belfast early in 2004 and stayed in my home over a couple of weekends, filming me as I went about the routine admin chores of my work – taking appointments by phone and answering emails – and interviewing me about my childhood and how I manage to integrate my psychic abilities into my daily life.

I explained to them about my spirit team and that I had a closer bond with them than most psychics and mediums. My team act as my guides not only in spiritual matters and communications but in practical ways on earth. If I have lost something at home, for instance, they will tell me where I've left it; when I'm in a strange place, such as a hotel room, they will describe the layout of my new surroundings and tell me where everything in the room – kettles, hairdryers and so on – is located. In other words they act as my eyes.

They have done this too on my journeys, in airports and at train stations. There have been times when airline staff have forgotten to collect me to help me board the aircraft and I've had to make my own way to the information desk to get help. My team will also warn me of obstacles when I am walking to and from the shops close to home. We really do work together at all times.

And though readings can be both physically and emotionally draining, chatting with my team on an everyday level is as natural as breathing and doesn't cost me any energy at all. There are those who may think I am imagining the bond with my team, but I have been able to prove that they can help me to find even the most mundane of things. Once, when I'd just arrived in my hotel room with my first Second Sight tour manager, Richard, I asked him to make a cup of tea. He looked around the room and gave up.

'There isn't anything to make tea with here,' he concluded and put the TV on.

I was desperate for my cuppa and turned to my team: 'Can't you just tell me where everything is and I'll do it myself?'

Steve came back straight away: 'Look below the TV – there's a cupboard there. Open it. The tea-making stuff is there.' And so it was, everything I needed.

Likewise, when I lose something at home, the team will tell me where to find it – 'It's sitting on the table in the dining room' or 'It's on your bed.'

※

A highlight of making the *Everyman* documentary was returning with the crew to film at my old school, Jordanstown. It was wonderful to meet some of my old teachers and to see how the school had changed in the twenty-four years since I had left. The staff told me that they were following my career with interest and congratulated me on my success.

The director of the film crew also wanted to show me in action, so I gave her a selection of the wide variety of emails I got regularly from people asking for my help, and one of these caught her attention. It came from a man who wanted an appointment with me because he felt he was suffering from auric intrusion. Ben had always been interested in spiritual and psychic phenomena and had heard of my work from a magazine article. His interest in the subject had resulted in him buying a number of books on psychic development, shortly after which he had started to suffer from symptoms similar to those Mark Hamilton had experienced. Unlike Mark, Ben could also hear voices talking to him.

Ben lived in Brighton, and it was my intention to arrange a meeting with him when I'd finished the documentary; it was important to be able to spend as much time as was needed to complete the treatment. But the *Everyman* director had other plans. She emailed Ben and asked him if he would be interested in having the treatment with me filmed. So, Ben and his mother came over for a weekend and stayed in my home. By this time, my apartment had become a little cramped, but with Ben and his mother in the guest room and the crew arranged on camp beds in the living room we just about managed to squeeze everyone in.

It turned out to be a very exhausting couple of days for me, both physically and mentally. The crew filmed Ben arriving at my flat and our first meeting. Then they filmed me carrying out the treatments on Ben, while at the same time asking me lots of questions about what I was doing. Finally, they filmed interviews with us, together and separately, about how the treatment was going. Altogether it was a pretty intense and intensive experience, not least because Ben's intruders were rather hostile.

Towards the end of the film, Ben remarked that since the treatment had begun he had started to feel normal again. Following further treatment with me back in Brighton he made a full recovery.

But that was only one part of the *Everyman* documentary. The next stage was to film me on tour, on location in Swindon, in Hastings and on Jersey.

This involved overnight stays, courtesy of the BBC for whom cost was clearly a significant factor. If anything, this convinced me that handling my own touring arrangements was far preferable. In one of the hotels, I got up to my room exhausted after a show, and I didn't need to be sighted to know my accommodation left a good deal to be desired. A strong odour of damp pervaded the room, but I was too tired to complain so slipped into bed still wearing my track suit. Before leaving the hotel I visited the Ladies only to find that it smelt disgusting, so I left quickly, feeling rather ill. Richard, my manager complained of feeling itchy for the rest of the day.

The shows themselves proved more tiring than usual because I had to be interviewed for the documentary before going on stage and again during the interval. I was very flattered to be making the documentary and enjoyed it thoroughly, but it was exhausting to be constantly observed on camera and filmed at every turn. And, of course, there was the frustration of knowing that a huge amount of the painstakingly made footage would not be used in the programme.

I loved my trip to Jersey even though it threw up an unexpected problem. It was my first visit there, so I hadn't realised that local business regulations were more complex than in the rest of the UK. Practising mediumship is considered a form of trading and therefore requires a licence under the Regulations of Undertaking (which govern who can trade). The day before my arrival I got a call from the promoter to say that the local council would not let me conduct private readings on the island unless I had a licence, which was a blow because we had planned to hold the readings in my hotel room and I already had a list of appointments lined up.

Time was too short to apply for a licence at that stage, so I rang around some of my Jersey clients and asked their advice. They recommended a couple who owned a health shop, the Bodhi Tree, and who already had a licence for events on their premises. The Bodhi Tree kindly agreed to come to my rescue, and I shall always be grateful to them for helping me out at short notice and with such a welcoming and convivial venue.

The film crew had arranged for me to do a reading for a couple who had agreed to have the session filmed. They were dubious about whether I could help and refused to tell the director anything about who they were or why they were there.

When the pair entered the room I was introduced to them and we joked companionably about Irish accents (the man was originally from Dublin). Then the reading got under way, and almost immediately, someone came through to me.

'I've got a gentleman here, who is trying to communicate,' I told them. 'He's quite young, maybe twenty-one or twenty-two, and passed on very suddenly. This is your son.'

At which point the man broke down.

'Your son says he is so sorry he didn't have the chance to say goodbye. His death was self-inflicted.' The lad went on to talk about the ring his father was wearing (which had belonged to the son), music that was important to the young man and being a cider drinker – evidence that I couldn't have known. The couple, who turned out to be the boy's father and stepmother, had not expected the reading to work at all and were overjoyed to have heard from their son. His father was especially comforted because he had been grieving for four years, since his son had died. It had been a particularly satisfying reading from my point of view and I was pleased that it had been captured on camera.

*

Working as a medium on television can be thrilling because you come across so many interesting people. In one programme, broadcast on UK Living, I appeared with other well-known UK psychics including Jacky Newcomb and Mia Dolan, and had to give a demonstration of mediumship to a studio audience as well as a live reading to a celebrity on each show. Live television can also be a bit nail-biting because you cannot rustle up a spirit to communicate with your celebrity at the drop of a hat; you are rather at the mercy of the spirit world. So far, thanks to my team, I have never failed to deliver even if I am not feeling particularly in the mood (and mediums do have their off days).

Television is quite a different environment from the kind of live shows we mediums usually give. Carrying out a proper demonstration on TV can be problematic because of the restrictions on what can be said and talked about. Viewers are generally unaware of this, and would no doubt be quite surprised to learn that we are not allowed to say we are talking to the dead or to use the word 'medium'. If I receive a message from someone who has committed suicide I am not permitted to mention the circumstances of the death; in fact no mention can be made of cause of death – heart attack, cancer – at all. We cannot give messages from anyone under eighteen years old, and certainly not from children who have passed on through miscarriage (the spirit exists from the moment of conception). This is so sad because a lot of people in an audience come because they want to hear from children.

Audiences aren't warned about these restrictions when they apply for tickets to attend the television studios, which seems very unfair to me. There should at least be some explanation before the show starts so the public is aware of why so little evidence can be passed on from the mediums.

If the authorities were to consider changes to the regulations – or just a relaxation of the restrictions on terminology – TV shows would come to life. As it is, it's impossible for mediums to relax completely because they have constantly to be aware of what they can and can't say. I can imagine my spirit team having to screen the people who want to communicate with their loved ones in the studio audience and explaining to them, 'Sorry, you can't come through because you're under eighteen,' or 'Sorry, you can't communicate because you don't fit the criteria laid down under the rules of the television authorities.'

To my mind, this is all utterly ridiculous and outdated, and certainly doesn't make for good television, let alone honest mediumship. Perhaps, if the people who came up with the rules went to a few demonstrations themselves, they might think twice about imposing such restrictions and appreciate the comfort that studio audiences and viewers draw from these shows, and what the consequences are if messages and message senders are censored.

While I was in the middle of one television demonstration I nearly made the mistake of giving a message from a little girl, who had passed on, to her mother who was in the studio audience.

'I have a little girl,' I said without thinking, before adding hastily to her mother, 'I'm so sorry, I can't pass this on at the moment. Can I talk to you after the show?'

The little girl couldn't understand why I wasn't able to let her mother know she was around. She thought it was her fault and that her mum didn't want to speak to her. Happily, I was able give her mother the message after the show.

CHAPTER 24

Reincarnation

———*———

One of the most fascinating stops on the Second Sight tours was York, in 2006. After the show there, I was introduced to the director of the city's Psychic Museum and, as I had a few days' break before my next show, he invited me to stay in York and visit the museum. I jumped at the chance.

The museum had been open for some three years (alas, it has now closed its doors due to lack of visitors) and was a fascinating place, designed also as a centre where members of the general public could check out their psychic potential in a safe environment. In small guided groups, visitors were given the opportunity to try their hand at telepathy, psychokinesis, dowsing, remote viewing and much more, including an aura machine that could take infrared photographs of the energy field surrounding people.

When I entered the building I could feel there was a lot of psychic activity, though this was to be expected in a property that dated back more than 600 years and had a lot of history. In fact the whole city of York is fascinating, famous for its ghosts and reputed to be the most haunted city in Britain. I would certainly concur with that. Over the next few days I was to have my fair share of paranormal experiences.

As I walked around the city I could see people in the narrow streets and alleys – people on the spirit side, that is, as I can't see anyone else. The spirit world is to me like the physical world is to a sighted person. If I am in an old building such as a pub or hotel I can watch the comings and goings of the spirit inhabitants. I don't have to meditate or be in a quiet environment to tune into the spirit world, it's my choice entirely whether or not I want to pick up on this activity. The only problem is that my spirit team has to keep people from trying to communicate with me, which was the case in York where the spirits sensed that I could see and hear them.

One evening, while we were crossing the street, I saw a woman walk straight out in front of a lorry. I froze in my steps. Why hadn't anyone tried to stop her? Of course, the people with me hadn't seen anything, and the accident had taken place on the astral and not the physical plane – if it had happened on the physical plane I wouldn't have been able to see it. But the incident – the screech of brakes and the screams of the woman – was so real and vivid that I thought it had happened right in front of us. Instead it had been a re-enactment from the past of a scene that was repeating itself because, as is the case so often with violent or sudden death, the woman had not yet moved on to the spirit world.

*

All this had taken place while we were making our way to York's famous Minster. The museum's director had taken me to a tactile (raised) map of the Minster so I could feel the outline and contours of the site, and although I had a nagging doubt about the wisdom of doing so, I wanted to pay the place a visit. My premonition was to be confirmed, for it was there that I received an interesting though disturbing personal revelation. As we drew level with the cathedral, I felt an overwhelming fear of going inside. I absolutely refused to put one foot inside the building, so we bypassed the Minster and continued on to the Psychic Museum.

I couldn't see the cathedral physically, yet I knew I'd been there before. I seemed to be picking up echoes of a past life and it wasn't a pleasant feeling. Nor were the echoes confined to York Minster; I was soon to learn that the premises of the Psychic Museum also had a part to play.

The director of the museum wanted to make a video of me going through its rooms and talking about what I was picking up. There was a slight delay in getting started, when for no apparent reason one of the video cameras wouldn't work – both cameras had been hired for the occasion and were brand new, but of course this failure of electrical equipment to function was rather to be expected on my part.

We got started with the remaining camera, and the director guided me through a warren of rooms while I described what I was detecting. In one particular room I sensed stained glass windows and had a strong feeling that this was a place where books had been written about the law or religious matters. I could see the volumes in my mind, and the writing in them looked unusual, fashioned with weird loops and shapes. It transpired that I was describing the calligraphy used at that time to record matters of importance.

This was an entirely new experience for me as there was no way

I could have known what the script looked like. I know the shape of some of the print letters of the alphabet as I briefly used a machine at college called an Opticon – a device with a camera that is placed on the page and transfers the printed words into tactile form so blind people can feel them – but I had never felt old-fashioned print.

Then, lying open on a table nearby, I saw a black book bound in leather, and reading from it was a man in the black clerical robes and high collar of a judge. The sight of both man and book filled me with dread. I knew instantly that this was a volume of law and that the reason for my fear was nothing less than my impending death. The man was checking facts in the book before passing sentence on me, and I knew instinctively that the book itself had been brought from the cathedral to this room for that purpose.

I was no longer in the present; I had been taken back to a previous life, a life in which I had been a man. A mixture of hate and rage welled up in me as I observed the judge running his fingers down the pages of the book. I had been accused of heresy against the Church, though I did not know what I was supposed to have said or done, only that the accusation was false. The man in black was ensuring there were no loopholes in his case before he announced the verdict on the following day. He was in control of the situation and I would have to accept my fate. The knowledge that there was no way I could convince him he was wrong – my situation was hopeless – turned my hatred and rage to despair.

Then I was standing in a tower room, a prisoner in the cathedral building, before the scene shifted again to a courtroom where I was waiting for the verdict. It was delivered quickly. I was to be hanged.

Suddenly, I was jolted back to the present by the sensation of choking, as if a rope was being pulled ever tighter around my throat. At first I didn't know where I was. Tears ran down my face at the intensity of the experience, yet I felt a sense of relief at having discovered why the book had filled me with such fear. The experience had been so traumatic, I felt unable to carry on and returned to my lodgings. But I was to come face to face once more with my accuser.

The next day we continued the tour of the museum building. As we were about to enter one of the rooms a figure stepped out in front of me and ordered me to stop. It was the same man who had been the arbiter of my downfall in that past life. I didn't think he'd melt away quite so easily, and he made it clear that he didn't want me to see any other part of the building. He was trying to dominate me again, but I wasn't having any of it. The tables had been turned. This time, he was in the spirit world and I had no fear of him nor was I going to take orders from him. My spirit team were with me and wanted to restrain him, but I wanted to talk to him and let him know that he was no longer in control. When I had explained this to him, he reluctantly stepped aside and let me continue on my way.

I will always remember my trip to York and have every intention of going back to conquer my fear of the Minster and go inside the building.

✳

Reincarnation is always a subject of keen interest and debate, and while opinions differ widely, I believe that, as individuals, we live many lifetimes on earth. There has been a good deal of evidence that proves this. People have been regressed under hypnosis and have been able to describe places and events of which they have no prior knowledge yet have been proven subsequently to exist.

I am convinced that many of our instincts and fears originate in our previous lives, although it is important not to attribute everything to past-life experiences. I also believe that the reason why we reincarnate is so that we might learn from our experiences in other lives and use the knowledge we have gained to help us on a soul level. Although we are not always aware of it, the accumulation of everything learned from all the lives we have lived is stored in the soul, that non-physical part of us that is sometimes called the 'higher self' and travels on into the spirit world when we die. While it isn't healthy to focus too much on what we have done in our past lives – we have enough to be getting on with in this life – if you are going through an issue that cannot be explained rationally then it might be beneficial to consult a past-life regressionist or a psychic who specialises in accessing past lives, as they should be able to find out whether the problem stems from a past life experience or not.

✳

York was not my first experience of being taken back to a past incarnation. I was in Manchester with friends some years earlier, when I was at Hethersett, and we had decided to visit the remains of an old amphitheatre to see if I could sense anything from it, but I got more than I bargained for.

Only the outer walls and the gate remained of the ancient site, no seats or any other indication as to what had taken place inside, yet as we entered the enclosure I felt a sense of deep unease creep over me. Within moments, the voices of the tourists around me faded out, to be replaced by the sound of trumpets and the shouts of a crowd. I was standing in the centre of a very different arena in a very different period of time – ancient Rome. Again I was a man, this time wearing the uniform of a gladiator.

Around me in the arena were other men, like me kitted out in the regalia of fighting men, and I knew that my orders from the Emperor were to fight them, but I also knew that this ran contrary to my sense of honour and justice – these were men who were still in training and my combat skills were far superior to theirs. I refused to fight. Nobody refused an order from the Emperor – who I knew was Nero – and he was not happy.

I was disgraced and stripped of my rank there and then, but worse still, my fate was placed in the hands of the crowd, which bayed for my blood, screaming for me to be put to death. But none of the other gladiators would fight me so it was decided that I should be killed by dogs instead. If I could survive their attack I would be a free man. The mastiffs were set loose, but there were too many for one man to fight off and I didn't stand a chance against them.

The sound of the shrieking crowds faded and I came to, lying on the ground in the centre of the Manchester amphitheatre on a hot summer's day. Everyone assumed that I had fainted from the heat.

It took me some time to rid my mind of those terrible images of the slavering dogs in the arena. Though I have grown up with dogs and have never been bitten or attacked by one, I've always had a fear of being too close to them, particularly when they are fighting, which is why I have never had a guide dog. I have a deep-rooted fear of my dog being attacked by another and of not being able to do anything to stop it. Once, when I was about ten, a dogfight started outside a shop I was in, and although they were nowhere near me, instinctively I leapt up on to the counter.

A few years after the Manchester experience, I went to visit the local Guide Dog Training Centre with my mobility officer. She took me through to the kennels so that I could meet one of the trainers. At the sight of the trainer, the dogs started barking excitedly, but I was terrified. We were standing in the centre of the kennels and, though I knew they were in their own individual kennels and were no threat to me, I felt as if I was surrounded by a pack of dogs. This fear of fighting dogs, I feel sure, has been carried forward from my incarnation as a gladiator and was instilled in me that day in that arena in Rome.

CHAPTER 25

Life's Journey

———*———

The more I tour, the more I love it — the places I visit, the strange adventures I've had and the people I meet. While the format of Second Sight is reassuringly familiar, the content is always excitingly different because the audience is never the same, even if the venue is. And I have never lost that feeling of awe and humility at the response I get across the country to my appearances. It is a privilege to be able to share my skills, to be the channel of messages from the spirit world, to be in a position to bring comfort to those who need it.

Looking back now, I don't regret not being able to 'see' the world as others see it. As I've said, far too much emphasis is placed on how we look rather than how we feel; because I rely on the other senses to be my guide, I view the world and the people I meet in an entirely different way.

But more than this, I am a great believer that things, both good and bad, happen for a purpose. I think of my blindness as a unique blessing. Everything that happened to me at my birth and during my early years was destined to be. I was meant to come into the world early. If I had not been premature I wouldn't have been blind, and if I hadn't been blind, I might not have developed my communication with the spirit world and my life would not, perhaps, have taken the unexpected path that it did. My survival at birth may have been a miracle, but as I grew up I gradually became aware that in my special gift a second miracle had been granted me.

My purpose is to use my gift to help people realise that life on earth is not the end, and that their loved ones who have passed on are still watching over them. I am convinced that one of the reasons why I was put on this earth was to be a conduit between this world and the spirit world, delivering evidence that life really does continue beyond death and passing on messages of comfort from loved ones in the spirit world. And because of my unusual combination of blindness and psychic gifts, I have been able to reach a wide audience and bring comfort to many people.

I may not be able to see the physical world, but I can see the pain of people who think their suffering is invisible to others; the anguish of mothers who have lost children; the grief of people who have lost loved ones or partners and feel they cannot go on without them. Sometimes I can see the future and am able to give people meaning and a reason to live when they feel hopeless and want to end it all. Some people say that I have saved their lives by being there to listen and give inspiration, and that's what I hope I will continue to do.

My life has been a journey and along the way I have experienced every form of emotion: grief, suffering, betrayal, anger, hopelessness and joy. But it has all been worth it because of the empathy it gives me for the work I am doing now. As a small baby, I had to fight to stay in the world, and everything that has happened to me since has made me stronger and more determined, and given me a greater understanding of what others are going through.

The most important lesson I have learned from my journey is that every situation, no matter how negative, will have a positive aspect, and that our emotional response to life's setbacks can also be transformed from negative to positive – hatred to love, anger to compassion.

Throughout my life, I have found that the right person has crossed my path at the right time – there has always been someone at the crossroads to give me a supporting nudge in the right direction. So, while my journey continues to unfold in extraordinary ways, I hope the story so far will lift you up when you are feeling down and inspire you to extend the hand of friendship to those you come across who might need a little support. If I can help just one person by writing this, then it will have been worth the effort.

Finally, I would like to give a few words of advice to those who have read this book. Be encouraged to follow in my footsteps. Live life with an adventurous spirit and a loving heart, see mistakes as achievements and remember that we all learn from them. Follow your destiny, live life to the full and have no regrets.

www.sharonnneill.com

Sharon Neill
PO Box 147
Newtonabbey BT36 5YH